STREAM OF CONSCIOUSNESS

IN THE MODERN NOVEL

Robert Humphrey

Stream of Consciousness in the Modern Novel

UNIVERSITY OF CALIFORNIA PRESS
Berkeley, Los Angeles, London

University of California Press
Berkeley and Los Angeles, California
University of California Press, Ltd.
London, England

ISBN: 0-520-00585-6
L. C. CATALOG CARD NO. 54-6673
Printed in the United States of America

10 11 12 13 14 15 16 17 18 19 20

Preface

STREAM OF CONSCIOUSNESS—what doesn't the phrase conjure up? Innermost confessions, wells of suppressed energy, daring experimentation, the passing fad, the welter of indiscrimination? Applied to the novel, it is, as Dorothy Richardson once said, a term characterized by its "perfect imbecility." But we have the term; it is ours. Our task now is to make it useful and meaningful, which means we have to come to some agreement on what it is; or, at the least, we need to have a fairly definite point of departure for intelligent discourse. The chapter titles of the following study indicate the focus of this modest contribution to such discourse. It will be noticed that three of the five chapters deal with problems of technique. In a sense, then, this study is a kind of manual of *how* to write stream-of-consciousness fiction, determined inductively rather than theoretically. Pervading the analysis of techniques, however, is something else; there is, for one thing, an appraisal of an important aspect of the contemporary literary scene; and for another, there is interpretation and evaluation of the novels and novelists taken as examples.

Dorothy Richardson, James Joyce, Virginia Woolf, and William Faulkner are the writers who appear most prominently in the following pages—not arbitrarily, but because they are, at once, important novelists and representative stream-of-consciousness writers. Clarity of illustration rather than variety and balance has been the deciding factor in choosing excerpts for examples. If Joyce steals many of the scenes, it is because he is most versatile and most skillful.

There will be many things remaining to be said about stream of consciousness in the modern novel. I have consciously avoided several interesting problems. The complexity of my subject dictated such limiting if my central task of clarifying a literary term was to be accomplished. I have not, therefore, investigated the historical antecedents and influences, except in passing to explain technical problems; nor have I made an attempt to catalogue fiction to determine finally what is and what is not stream of consciousness; and finally, with more regret, I have minimized philosophical speculation.

Many acknowledgments are in order; the following persons I wish to thank publicly:

Leon Howard, to whom the book is dedicated—a slight gesture compared to the rare dedication he proffers to his students;

Leonard Unger, that true colleague, for suggestions and encouragement; Harry and Mary Frissell, for aid in preparing the manuscript; Mr. Glenn Gosling and Mr. James Kubeck, of the University of California Press, for kind and wise editorial aid; Dean Russell and the Research Council, Louisiana State University, for generous financial assistance.

I wish to thank the following publishers who have permitted me to quote from copyrighted materials: Alfred A. Knopf, Inc., for *Pilgrimage* by Dorothy Richardson; The Viking Press, Inc., for *Portrait of the Artist as a Young Man* by James Joyce; Random House, Inc., for *Ulysses* by James Joyce, for *The Sound and the Fury* and *As I Lay Dying* by William Faulkner, and for *World Enough and Time* by Robert Penn Warren; and Harcourt, Brace and Co., for *Mrs. Dalloway* by Virginia Woolf and for *All the King's Men* by Robert Penn Warren. Parts of chapters 1 and 4 have appeared in modified form in *Philological Quarterly* and *The University of Kansas City Review*.

ROBERT HUMPHREY

Louisiana State University
September, 1953

Contents

1

The Functions

> *The discovery that memories, thoughts, and feelings exist outside the primary consciousness is the most important step forward that has occurred in psychology since I have been a student of that science.*
>
> WILLIAM JAMES

STREAM OF CONSCIOUSNESS is one of the delusive terms which writers and critics use. It is delusive because it sounds concrete and yet it is used as variously—and vaguely—as "romanticism," "symbolism," and "surrealism." We never know whether it is being used to designate the bird of technique or the beast of genre—and we are startled to find the creature designated is most often a monstrous combination of the two. The purpose of this study is to examine the term and its literary implications.

Stream of Consciousness Defined

Stream of consciousness is properly a phrase for psychologists. William James coined it.[1] The phrase is most clearly useful when it is applied to mental processes, for as a rhetorical locution it becomes doubly metaphorical; that is, the word "consciousness" as well as the word "stream" is figurative, hence, both are less precise and less stable. If, then, the term stream of consciousness (I shall use it since it is already established as a literary label) is reserved for indicating an approach to the presentation of *psychological* aspects of character in fiction,

1

it can be used with some precision. This reservation I shall make, and it is the basis from which the contradicting and often meaningless commentary on the stream-of-consciousness novel can be resolved.[2]

The stream-of-consciousness novel is identified most quickly by its subject matter. This, rather than its techniques, its purposes, or its themes, distinguishes it. Hence, the novels that are said to use the stream-of-consciousness *technique* to a considerable degree prove, upon analysis, to be novels which have as their essential subject matter the consciousness of one or more characters; that is, the depicted consciousness serves as a screen on which the material in these novels is presented.

"Consciousness" should not be confused with words which denote more restricted mental activities, such as "intelligence" or "memory." The justifiably irate comments of the psychology scholars deplore the layman's use of the term. One of these scholars writes: "It has been said that no philosophical term is at once so popular and so devoid of standard meaning as *consciousness;* and the layman's usage of the term has been credited with begging as many metaphysical questions as will probably be the privilege of any single word."[3] The area which we are to examine here is an important one in which this confusion has been amassed. Since our study will concern persons who are laymen in psychology, it is necessary that we proceed with the "layman's usage." Naturally, the stream-of-consciousness writers have not defined their label. We readers who have stamped it on them must try to do it.

Consciousness indicates the entire area of mental attention, from preconsciousness on through the levels of the mind up to and including the highest one of rational, communicable awareness.[4] This last area is the one with which almost all psychological fiction is concerned. Stream-of-consciousness fiction differs from all other psychological fiction precisely in that it is concerned with those levels that are more inchoate than rational verbalization—those levels on the margin of attention.

So far as stream-of-consciousness fiction is concerned, it is pointless to try to make definite categories of the many levels of consciousness. Such attempts demand the answers to serious metaphysical questions, and they put serious questions about the stream-of-consciousness writers' concepts of psychology and their aesthetic intentions—questions which the epistemologists, the psychologists, and the literary historians have not yet answered satisfactorily. It is desirable for an analysis of stream-of-consciousness fiction to assume that there are levels of consciousness from the lowest one just above oblivion to the highest one which is represented by verbal (or other formal) communication. "Low" and "high" simply indicate degrees of the rationally ordered. The adjectives "dim" and "bright" could be used just as well to indicate these degrees. There are, however, two levels of consciousness which can be rather simply distinguished: the "speech level" and the "prespeech level." There is a point at which they overlap, but otherwise the distinction is quite clear. The prespeech level, which is the concern of most of the literature under consideration in this study, involves no communicative basis as does the speech level (whether spoken or written). This is its salient distinguishing characteristic. In short, the prespeech levels of consciousness are not censored, rationally controlled, or logically ordered. By "consciousness," then, I shall mean the whole area of mental processes, including especially the prespeech levels. The term "psyche" I shall use as a synonym for "consciousness," and at times, even the word "mind" will serve as another synonym. These synonyms, although they are handicapped by the various evocative qualities they possess, are convenient to use because they lend themselves well to the forming of adjectives and adverbs.

Hence, "consciousness" must not be confused with "intelligence" or "memory" or any other such limiting term. Henry James has written novels which reveal psychological processes in which a single point of view is maintained so that the entire novel is presented through the intelligence of a character. But these, since they do not deal at all with prespeech levels of consciousness, are not what I have defined as stream-of-consciousness novels. Marcel Proust has written a modern classic which is often cited as an example of stream-of-consciousness fiction,[5] but *A la recherche du temps perdu* is concerned only with the reminiscent aspect of consciousness. Proust was deliberately recapturing the past for the purposes of communication; hence he did not write a stream-of-consciousness novel. Let us think of consciousness as being in the form of an iceberg—the whole iceberg and not just the relatively small surface portion. Stream-of-consciousness fiction is, to follow this comparison, greatly concerned with what lies below the surface.

With such a concept of consciousness, we may define stream-of-consciousness fiction as a type of fiction in which the basic emphasis is placed on exploration of the prespeech levels of consciousness for the purpose, primarily, of revealing the psychic being of the characters.

When some of the novels which fall into this classification are considered, it becomes immediately apparent that the techniques by which the subjects are controlled and the characters are presented are palpably different from one novel to the next. Indeed, there is no stream-of-consciousness technique. Instead, there are several quite different techniques which are used to present stream of consciousness.

The Self-conscious Mind

It is not an uncommon misconception that many modern novels, and particularly the ones that are generally labeled stream of consciousness, rely greatly upon private symbols to represent private confusions. The misconception comes primarily from considering whatever is "internal" or "subjective" in characterization as arrant fantasy, or, at best, as psychoanalytical.[6] Serious misreadings and unsound evaluations result from this initial misunderstanding, particularly in discussion of major twentieth-century novels. I refer to such subjective fiction as *Ulysses, Mrs. Dalloway, To the Lighthouse,* and *The Sound and the Fury.* These novels may very well be within a category we can label stream of consciousness, so long as we know what we are talking about. The evidence reveals that we never do—or never have done so.

It is meaningless to label all of the novels stream of consciousness that are generally named as such, unless we mean by that phrase simply "inner awareness." The expression of this quality is what they have in common. It is, however, apparent that that is not what has been meant when they have been so labeled and forced to share the same categorical niche. It is not what William James meant when he coined the term. James was formulating psychological theory and he had discovered that "memories, thoughts, and feelings exist outside the primary consciousness" and, further, that they appear to one, not as a chain, but as a stream, a flow.[7] Whoever, then, first applied the phrase to the novel did so correctly only if he was thinking of a *method* of representing inner awareness. What has actually happened is that *monologue intérieur* was clumsily translated into English. But it is palpably true that the methods of the novels in which this device is used are different, and that there are dozens of other novels which use internal monologue which no one would seriously classify as stream of consciousness. Such are, for example, *Moby Dick, Les Faux-monnayeurs,* and *Of Time and the River.* Stream of consciousness, then, is not a synonym for *monologue intérieur.* It is not a term to name a particular method or technique; although it probably was used originally in literary criticism for that purpose. One can safely conjecture that such a loose and fanciful term was a radiant buoy to well-meaning critics who had lost their bearings. The natural, and historically accurate, association of the term with psychology, along with the overwhelming psychoanalytical trend of twentieth-century thought, has resulted in giving all novels that could be loosely associated with the loose phrase "stream of consciousness" a marked Viennese accent.

The word "stream" need not concern us immediately, for representation of the flow of consciousness is, provided one is convinced that consciousness flows, entirely a matter of technique. The approach to take is to consider the word "consciousness" and to attempt to formulate what, to the various writers, is the ultimate significance of what consciousness contains. It is, in short, a psychological and a philosophical question. Stream-of-consciousness literature is psychological literature, but it must be studied at the level on which psychology mingles with epistemology. Immediately the question confronts us: What does consciousness contain? Then, too, what does it contain so far as philosophy and psychology have investigated it *and* what does it contain so far as the novelists in question have represented it? These may be mutually exclusive questions; they are certainly different ones. But the concern here is not with psychological theory; it is with novelistic subject matter. The question for this study is a phenomenological one: What does consciousness contain in the sense of what has it contained so far as the consciousness of the novelists have experienced it? Any answer must respect the possible range of a creative writer's sensitivity and imagination. No answer needs proving beyond the gesture of saying: There it is in Virginia Woolf; there it is in James Joyce. It should be remembered that, first, we are attempting to clarify a literary term; and second, we are trying to determine how fictional art is enriched by the depiction of inner states.

The attempt to create human consciousness in fiction is a modern attempt to analyze human nature. Most of us will be convinced, now, that it can be the starting point of that most important of all intellectual functions. We have, for example, Henry James's word for it that "experience is never limited, and it is never complete." He continues in the same context to point to the "chamber of consciousness" as the chamber of experience.[8] Consciousness, then, is *where* we are aware of human experience. And this is enough for the novelist. He, collectively, leaves nothing out: sensations and memories, feelings and conceptions, fancies and imaginations—and those very unphilosophic, but consistently unavoidable phenomena we call intuitions, visions, and insights. These last terms, which usually embarrass the epistemologist, unlike the immediately preceding series, are not always included under the label "mental life." Precisely for this reason it is important to point them up here. Human "knowledge" which comes not from "mental" activity but from "spiritual" life is a concern of novelists, if not of psychologists. Knowledge, then, as a category of consciousness must include intuition, vision, and sometimes even the occult, so far as twentieth-century writers are concerned.

Thus, we may, on inductive grounds, conclude that the realm of life with which stream-of-consciousness literature is concerned is mental and spiritual experience—both the whatness and the howness of it. The whatness includes the categories of mental experiences: sensations, memories, imaginations, conceptions, and intuitions. The howness includes the symbolizations, the feelings, and the processes of association. It is often impossible to separate the what from the how. Is, for example, memory a part of mental content or is it a mental process? Such fine distinctions, of course, are not the concern of novelists as novelists. Their object, if they are writing stream of consciousness, is to enlarge fictional art by depicting the inner states of their characters.

The problem of character depiction is central to stream-of-consciousness fiction. The great advantage, and consequently the best justification of this type of novel, rests on its potentialities for presenting character more accurately and more realistically. There is the example of the *roman expérimental* behind James Joyce, Virginia Woolf, and Dorothy Richardson, and though a little farther removed, behind William Faulkner. But there is a difference, and it is a tremendous one, between Zola and Dreiser, say, two novelists who attempted a kind of laboratory method in fiction, and the stream-of-consciousness writers. It is indicated chiefly in the difference in subject matter—which is, for the earlier novelists, motive and action (external man) and for the later ones, psychic existence and functioning (internal man). The difference is also revealed in the psychological and philosophical thinking in back of this. Psychologically it is the distinction between behavioristic concepts and psychoanalytical ones; philosophically, it is that between a broad materialism and a generalized existentialism. Combined, it is the difference between being concerned about what one does and being concerned about what one is.

I do not offer a Freudian or Existential brief for stream-of-consciousness literature. All of its authors doubtless were familiar, more or less, with psychoanalytical theories and with the twentieth-century recrudescence of personalism and were directly or indirectly influenced by them. Even more certain can we be that these writers were influenced by the broader concepts of a "new psychology" and a "new philosophy"—a nebulous label for all postbehavioristic and nonpositivistic thinking, including any philosophy or psychology which emphasized man's inner mental and emotional life (e.g., Gestalt psychology, psychoanalytical psychology, Bergsonian ideas of *durée* and the *élan vital,* religious mysticism, much symbolic logic, Christian existentialism, etc.). It is this background which led to the great difference between Zola's subject matter and Joyce's; between Balzac's and Dorothy Richardson's. Yet as novelists all of these writers were concerned with the problem of characterization. There is naturalism in character depiction found in the work of both the late and the early of the above novelists, but there is a contrast and it is determined by the difference in psychological focusing. In short, the stream-of-consciousness novelists were, like the naturalists, trying to depict life accurately; but unlike the naturalists, the life they were concerned with was the individual's psychic life.

In examining the chief stream-of-consciousness writers in order to discover their diverse evaluations of inner awareness, we need to keep in mind two important questions: What can be accomplished by presenting character as it exists psychically? How is fictional art enriched by the depiction of inner states? The direction of the following discussion will be toward answering these questions.

Impressions and Visions

Unlike most originators of artistic genres, the twentieth-century pioneer in stream of consciousness remains the least well-known of the important stream-of-consciousness writers. It is the price a writer pays, even an experimental writer, for engendering monotony. Readers may justifiably neglect Dorothy Richardson, but no one who would understand the development of twentieth-century fiction can. With a great debt to Henry James and Joseph Conrad, she invented the fictional depiction of the flow of consciousness. Sometimes she is brilliant; always she is sensitive to the subtleties of mental functioning; but finally, she becomes lost in the overflow—a formless, unending deluge of realistic detail.

It is difficult to grasp Dorothy Richardson's aims. She gives this account of them herself in the brilliant foreword to *Pilgrimage:*

> . . . the present writer, proposing at this moment to write a novel and looking around for a contemporary pattern, was faced with the choice between following one of her regiments and attempting to produce a feminine equivalent of the current masculine realism. Choosing the latter alternative, she

presently set aside, at the bidding of a dissatisfaction that revealed its nature without cause, a considerable mass of manuscript. Aware, as she wrote, of the gradual falling away of the preoccupations that for a while had dictated the briskly moving script, and of the substitution, for these inspiring preoccupations, *of a stranger in the form of contemplated reality having for the first time in her experience its own say, and apparently justifying those who acclaim writing as the surest means of discovering the truth about one's own thoughts* and beliefs, she had been at the same time increasingly tormented, not only by the failure, of this now so independently assertive reality, adequately to appear within the text, but by its revelation, whencesoever focused, of a hundred faces, any one of which, the moment it was entrapped within the close mesh of direct statement, summoned its fellows to disqualify it.[9]

The italics are mine and the words they emphasize reveal just what a reader gets from *Pilgrimage*. It is a psychical autobiography, which means that it is almost impossible for a reader to be empathic toward it or to understand the importance of its implications. It is difficult to see either a microcosm or an exemplum here. There is a certain amount of universal interest possible in looking in on how a fairly sensitive but greatly limited mind functions and in discovering how it classifies and rejects; and there is even an interest in discovering what a great amount of dullness a mind encounters in the world—but such an interest is not likely to last throughout twelve volumes. The one possibility left for Dorothy Richardson was to reveal some of the mysteries of psychic life, to depict it as an area from which something of the external world could be explained. But this she does not do. She does not investigate the world of consciousness on a level that is deep enough.

Two interpretations of *Pilgrimage* have suggested a

thematic significance in the work: John Cowper Powys, Dorothy Richardson's most persuasive admirer, justifies her novel because it is a presentation of the feminine view of life, which he is convinced is a worth-while thing in itself, necessary to supplement the masculine picture of things.[10] Dorothy Richardson herself evidently believed this also. She says, we recall, that she began writing in order "to produce a feminine equivalent of the current masculine realism." Unfortunately, the dichotomy between the feminine and masculine viewpoints is too tenuous, if not wholly inadequate, for any degree of profundity. Granted a possible over-all difference between these two classes of attitudes, still the basic problems and situations of life (hence of art) are neither masculine nor feminine, but simply human. One might as well propose that Faulkner writes in order to present a psychotic equivalent of the current sane realism! Faulkner has, certainly, advantages, which we shall consider presently, in presenting life from an abnormal person's point of view—and likewise there are certain values inherent in the presentation of life from a feminine point of view—but these values cannot be realized in a vacuum. An adequate purpose is not found in presenting these viewpoints merely for the sake of novelty. It is hardly justified, at least, for important literature. Another critic, Joseph Warren Beach, thinks of *Pilgrimage* as a quest story. He believes the point of the novel lies in Miriam's continuous search for a symbolic "little coloured garden," and again that she is on a pilgrimage "to some elusive shrine, glimpsed here and there and lost to view." This theory is easily credible, and it gives an important justification to the novel; but as Beach intimates, how digressive, how vague, and how long![11]

Dorothy Richardson deserves more credit as a pioneer in novelistic method than as a successful creator of fiction. There are indications that the pioneering fever was the conscious impetus, for the opening chapters of *Pilgrimage* were "written to the accompaniment of a sense of being upon a fresh pathway, an adventure so searching and, sometimes, so joyous as to produce a longing for participation."[12] By "participation" Dorothy Richardson meant "readers"; but I suspect she will always be rather bland hors d'oeuvres for the reading public. However, another kind of participation came. Dorothy Richardson recognizes this, too, in her foreword: "The lonely track, meanwhile, had turned out to be a populous highway. Amongst those who had simultaneously entered it, two figures stood out. One a woman mounted upon a magnificently caparisoned charger, the other a man walking, with eyes devoutly closed, weaving as he went a rich garment of new words wherewith to clothe the antique dark material of his engrossment." The woman we take to be Virginia Woolf; the man, who is described more aptly, is certainly James Joyce. There is little difficulty in determining why either of these writers used stream-of-consciousness methods.

Virginia Woolf speaks eloquently as a critic herself, and the key to her purposes is in her critical writing. Less eloquently, though authoritatively, are her purposes spoken by a number of other critics, partly because she gives them the key and partly because she lucidly reveals in her novels what she is about. Since Virginia Woolf's accomplishments have been so thoroughly analyzed,[13] it is necessary here only to summarize in order to provide a direct answer to the question which is in front of us: For what purpose does this writer use stream of consciousness?

Let us answer the question at once and show afterward why we have come to the answer. Virginia Woolf wanted to formulate the possibilities and processes of inner realization of truth—a truth she reckoned to be inexpressible; hence only on a level of the mind that is not expressed could she find this process of realization functioning. At least this is true with her three stream-of-consciousness novels. The first two of these, *Mrs. Dalloway* and *To the Lighthouse,* can be considered together, since they illustrate in only slightly different ways the same achievement. *The Waves* marks a different approach.

Clarissa Dalloway, Mrs. Ramsay, and Lily Briscoe all have moments of vision. Not that they are disciplined mystics who have prepared themselves for this, but their creator believed that the important thing in human life is the search the individual constantly has for meaning and identification. The fulfillment of her characters is therefore achieved when Virginia Woolf feels they are ready to receive the vision. The novels are a record of their preparations for the final insight. The preparations are in the form of fleeting insights into other characters and syntheses of present and past private symbols.

We know from Virginia Woolf's essays that she believed the important thing for the artist to express is his private vision of reality, of what life, subjectively, is. She thought that the search for reality is not a matter of dramatic external action. "Examine an ordinary mind on an ordinary day," she says, and again: "Life is . . . a luminous halo, a semi-transparent envelope surrounding us from the beginning of consciousness to the end. Is is not the task of the novelists to convey this varying, this unknown and uncircumscribed spirit . . . ?"[14] Thus the search, thought Virginia Woolf, is a psychic activity, and it is the preoccupation (it surrounds us) of most human beings. The only thing is that most human beings are not aware of this psychic activity, so deep down is it in their consciousness. This is one of the reasons Virginia Woolf chose characters who are extraordinarily sensitive, whose psyches would at least occasionally be occupied with this search. And it is, above all, the reason that she chose the stream-of-consciousness medium for her most mature presentation of this theme.

Analogically, we may call the Virginia Woolf of these two stream-of-consciousness novels a mystic. She is a mystic in that she is interested in the search her characters'make for unification. The climax of *Mrs. Dalloway* suggests the mystic's search for cosmic identification. And what, in the novel, is more nearly the mystic's vision of light than Lily Briscoe's crucial attainment of vision in *To the Lighthouse?* It is because this novelist is building up to the moments of illumination that her method is one of presenting psychic impressions. She selects these impressions as stages toward arriving at a vision. It is not the undifferentiated trivia that impinge on consciousness which interest her; it is the illusive event that is meaningful and that carries the germ of the final insight.

The Waves is a different kind of accomplishment. In this novel there is no mystical quest after identity and subjective essence; it is a presentation of the purest psychological analysis in literature. Not, let it be noted, of psychoanalysis. Spontaneous psychic life is presented in this novel. The achievement is the tracing of the growth of psychic lives. The method is as much the presentation of uncensored observations by the characters of each other as it is of the characters' own psychological make-up. Indeed, the two are the same thing in this "X-ray of intuition," as Bernard Blackstone labels it.

The psychic anatomy here is not a bare analysis, however. It is full of the impressionist's sensitivity to color, sound, and shapes as Virginia Woolf's earlier novels are. The formal soliloquies are close to poetry in their concentrated quality, their dependence on rhythms, and their exact diction. This work is the most eloquent of this eloquent novelist's fiction. It is also the most uncommunicative, for here Virginia Woolf's private sense of the significant is confined to characters who remain only individuals and never compose into universal symbols. Reality is the aim and it is achieved, but the rich symbolic significance of the characters of the two earlier stream-of-consciousness novels is lacking. As much as we may admire and enjoy this work, we are almost bound to agree with David Daiches that it is overloaded with technique.

A person much more often charged with such artistic trammeling is James Joyce. In creative productions the ends justify the means, and Joyce has contributed hugely to a revitalized fiction. What the ends of *Ulysses* finally are, I do not expect to determine. The many volumes which have been written to explain Joyce's purposes threaten the cursory appraisal; but I should like at least to suggest one important achievement of Joyce's in *Ulysses* which is central to his whole purpose and which is greatly dependent on stream-of-consciousness techniques. This is the marvelous degree of objectivity which he achieves. Joyce, more than any other novelist, gains what Joseph Warren Beach terms "dramatic immediacy." In *A Portrait of the Artist as a Young Man,* Joyce, in the guise of Stephen, states his theory of the evolution of artistic form when he maintains that "the personality of the artist, at first a cry or a cadence or a mood and then a fluid and lambent narrative, finally refines itself out of existence, impersonalizes itself, so to speak. The esthetic image in the dramatic form is life purified in and projected from the human imagination. The mystery of esthetic like that of material creation is accomplished. The artist, like the God of the creation, remains within or behind or beyond or above his handiwork, invisible, refined out of existence, indifferent, paring his fingernails."[15] The author is almost "refined out of existence" in *Ulysses.* Why does Joyce place such an important emphasis on ridding his work of signs of its author? As a feat in itself it would be nothing more than an interesting tour de force. The effect of this great accomplishment is to make the reader feel he is in direct contact with the life represented in the book. It is a method for doing what Joyce wanted to do, and that is to present life as it actually is, without prejudice or direct evaluations. It is, then, the goal of the realist and the naturalist. The thoughts and actions of the characters are there, as if they were created by an invisible, indifferent creator. We must accept them, because they exist.

If Joyce's accomplishment is, then, that of the most successful of realists, what is his aim? What view of life can he communicate by impersonalizing his creation through presenting the direct interior monologues of his characters? The answer is this—and it is from this basis that a future evaluation of *Ulysses* must start: for Joyce, existence is a comedy and man is to be satirized, gently not bitterly, for his incongruous and pitiful central role in it. The objective distance of the author, working as it chiefly does in *Ulysses* on the level of man's daydreams and mental delusions, shows the smallness of man, the great disparity between his ideals and his actualities, and the prosaicness of most of the things he considers special. Joyce's methods point to this: the *Odyssey* pattern is a means for equating the heroic and the ordinary, and the undifferentiated internal monologue is a means for equating the trivial and the profound. Life is depicted by Joyce so minutely that there is no room for any values to stand out. Joyce presents life with its shortcomings and its inherent contradictions, and the result is satire. Only within stream of consciousness could the necessary objectivity be attained for making it all convincingly realistic; for the pathos is in the fact that *man* thinks he is special and heroic, not that *Joyce* thinks he is pitiful.

Joyce is a writer of comedy and of satiric comedy at that. He is not a jokester or a funny man. The novel is not as a whole, in any sense, a hoax: the overtones are too far-reaching; there is too credible a concept of man's psychic life presented. It is obvious, however, that *Ulysses* is, fundamentally, a satirical comment on modern man's life. Joyce could never have shown this convincingly with any subject other than man's life on the level of consciousness, where the ideal can be reached for, even by the everyman Leopold Bloom, whose very next act or thought will show how far he actually is from it.[16]

The only other writer who utilizes effectively this natural advantage for satire in depiction of psyche is William Faulkner. But there is a difference. Faulkner, although he makes wide use of comic materials, is not a writer of comedy, not even of divine comedy. Faulkner's satires of circumstance are, like those of the Hardy of *Jude the Obscure* and the poems, irrevocably tragic. And they are more profound than Joyce's. One way to explain this is to consider Faulkner as a stream-of-consciousness writer who combines the views of life of Woolf with those of Joyce. Faulkner's views are not the same in either case; but the cast is similar in both. His characters search for insight, and their search is fundamentally ironic.

Since relatively little study has been published on Faulkner, it is necessary to consider his accomplishments more thoroughly than we have those of the other writers. It is tempting to go afield in doing this, but we shall try to focus on answering that question which underlies the present study: Why does Faulkner choose to deal with psychic processes in *The Sound and the Fury* and *As I Lay Dying*? One commentator has it that Faulkner, in the former novel, which we shall consider first, was trying to depict the Freudian idea of dream mechanism and consequently was dealing with unconscious manifestations of libido activity.[17] This certainly, if valid, would automatically put the novel in the stream-of-consciousness genre—if, that is, it could produce a work of art at all. Another writer decides that since the date of the Benjy episode is an Easter Sunday, Benjy is a Christ symbol, etc., which puts the novel I don't know where.[18] These interpretations may be discarded because they involve the heresies of dehumanization, which Faulkner must hate more than anything else. Three much more convincing and sensible critics agree on the basic proposition that all of Faulkner's work can be interpreted on a basis of broad myth and related symbolism. The principle of this interpretation is that Faulkner's entire work is a dramatization, in terms of myth, of the social conflict between the sense of ethical responsibilities in traditional humanism and the amorality of modern naturalism (animalism) in Faulkner, in the South, and by extension, I suppose, universally.[19]

If we begin with this principle as a basis for interpretation of *The Sound and the Fury,* we can understand that the novel is another chapter in the history of the collapse of the humanism of the Sartoris (here Compson) family in a world of the animalism of the Snopeses. The chief character symbol of the Sartoris-Compson code is Quentin III, who commits suicide; the symbol of the Snopes code is Jason IV (actually a Sartoris-Compson), who collapses most completely in that he embraces Snopesism. The other characters represent symbolically stages in degeneracy of, and escape from, the Sartoris-Compson code: Benjy by inherited idiocy; Candace by sexual promiscuity; Mr. Compson by rhetoric and liquor; Mrs. Compson by invalidism; Maury by liquor and laziness. The main conflict then is focused on Quentin and Jason, protagonists respectively of Sections II and III of the novel. But Section I has Benjy as the center of things. The reason for this is that Benjy, with an idiot's mind, is able to present the necessary exposition in not only its simplest tragic terms, but also in terms of symbols, which because they are from an idiot's mind are conveniently general in their meaning and are therefore flexible. It must be remembered, too, that Faulkner saw idiocy as a possible way for a Sartoris-Compson to escape the ethical rigor of a code that depends on exertion of intellect and will. Benjy's role, then, is both to reflect an aspect of Compson degeneracy and to introduce the terms of the main conflict with the simple, forceful symbols available to an idiot.

This conflict is centered on Quentin. Thus the central episode of the novel, which concerns him, is the crucial one. Quentin is determined to preserve the Sartoris-Compson traditions of humanism—in terms of the honor of the Compsons. His obsession is with his sister Candace, who has given in to Snopesism sexually; but Quentin must not accept the fact of her promiscuity, for to him, her honor is a symbol of the dying honor of the Compsons. He convinces himself that he is the violator of Candace's chastity. This conviction is finally without effect because no one else believes him. Eventually Quentin has to accept his defeat and recognition of the Compson defeat. Unable to stand this, he, too, escapes—by suicide.

Faulkner's method puts the struggle in terms of Quentin's psychic conflict, for it is on a prespeech level of mental life that his actual defeat comes—his consciousness defeats him. He can escape everything (he goes to Harvard and he is a gentleman) except his knowledge of the truth. He even attempts to escape his consciousness of the factual world (he takes the hands off his watch; he attempts a substitute for his sister with the little Italian girl), but the only way to do this is by death. In an important sense, then, it is Quentin's consciousness that is his antagonist.

It is almost enough to submit that the advantages of the stream-of-consciousness method for this novel are explained by the central role consciousness itself plays in it. However, we might suggest here the advantages stream-of-consciousness fiction has in presenting symbols as substitutes for rationally formulated ideas. This can be illustrated in both the Benjy and Quentin sections of the novel. The two kinds of mental aberration represented reveal themselves naturally in terms of images and symbols. Because they are represented as coming directly from a premeditative stage of conscious activity, they carry a convincingness and a fuller impact than they otherwise would. The three symbols that signify everything for Benjy (firelight, the pasture, and Candace) are used so frequently that they come to dominate not only Benjy's consciousness, but the reader's also. Yet, such repetition has a naturalness about it because it comes from a mind as simple as Benjy's is. With Quentin, mental simplicity is not the thing; but obsession tends to give the same effect. Here the significance of the odor-of-honeysuckle image, the wedding announcement symbol, and all of the other symbol or image motifs grows in importance simply by the frequent repetition, which repetition is quite natural to an obsessed mind.

On a more immediate basis, the use of stream-of-consciousness techniques is appropriate in this novel because of the fundamental problem involved in describing an idiot or an obsessed person with any objectivity. Faulkner, among others, has done it out of a stream-of-consciousness context (in *The Hamlet, Wild Palms,* etc.), but never has he been able to get the objective distance necessary to prevent either a bizarre or farcical marring of it except in his stream-of-consciousness novels.

An additional effect Faulkner achieves is a contrast in *not* using stream-of-consciousness techniques in the last two episodes of the novel. It is in these sections that Jason's side of the story is presented. The techniques are soliloquy and conventional omniscient narration, with little attempt to present unspoken thoughts. The meaning this change of technique carries is that Jason's acceptance of the amoral Snopesian world is complete—it pervades his whole mental life; hence on the level of psychic life with which the novel had been dealing, there is no conflict for Jason. His conflicts are entirely in the material world of things and acts, not in the ideal one of thoughts.

So, it would seem on first consideration, are those of the characters in Faulkner's other stream-of-consciousness novel, *As I Lay Dying.* The poverty stricken, ignorant, hill folk presented there are, however, not Snopeses, despite their Snopes-like qualities of hypocrisy, promiscuity, and avarice. The macabre pilgrimage to bury the dead, which is the central subject of the novel, is motivated by a sense of duty and honor as rigid as any the Sartoris-Compsons might have.

As I Lay Dying is, then, a marginal work in the Faulkner canon. It functions in relation to the whole Snopes-Sartoris drama as a device for repetition on a lighter scale—a minor parallel theme, so to speak. It deals with neither Snopeses nor Sartorises, but it does deal with the question of ethical codes. The method of presentation involves showing the contrast of the Snopes-like external lives of the Bundrens (the selfishness of Anse, the promiscuity of Dewey Dell, etc.) with the Sartoris-like rigidity of their internal sense of form and moral obligation (the fortitude of Addie, the persistence in duty in Cash, the heroism and loyalty of Jewel, etc.). Through the use of soliloquy to present stream of consciousness, this inner aspect of these hill people is eloquently established. Their humanism is primitive and distorted, but it is as rigid and moral as that of the Sartoris clan; and their animalism is as ugly and perverse as is that of the Snopeses—but there is ignorance, not amorality, at the base.

Stream-of-consciousness fiction is essentially a technical feat. Its successful working-out depended on technical resources exceeding those of any other type of fiction. Because this is so, any study of the genre must be essentially an examination of method. A study of devices and form becomes significant if we understand the achievement that justifies all of the virtuosity. Stream of consciousness is not technique for its own sake. It is based on a realization of the force of the drama that takes place in the minds of human beings.

One writer saw it as metaphysically significant, and her own predilections for the reality of visions led her to demonstrate the insight which the ordinary mind is capable of. For Virginia Woolf, the fleeting but vital visions of the human mind had to be expressed within the setting of that mind—and she was right; for she alone has been able to communicate precisely that sense of vision. Another writer saw it as high comedy, and he saw that it was pitiful too. Joyce's insight into man's mind was complemented by an equal insight into man's surface actions. The juxtaposition of the two was material for comedy, because the comparison between man's aspirations and his achievements was for Joyce the stuff of the comic: incongruity so great it could not produce tears, and if one were as faithless as Joyce was, it could not produce visions either. Faulkner saw one aspect of the drama as a tragedy of blood. (In other aspects he saw it as comedy, both high and low.) "The mind, mind has mountains" Faulkner might say; and he would have to add that the human being usually falls from the sheer cliffs to destruction. The tragedy of being conscious of a dying way of life, and the abortive attempts of the mind to lead the individual to isolation from the materials of a decaying reality gave Faulkner his themes. These come to the reader most forcibly in that writer's stream-of-consciousness novels, where the scene can be the one in which the tragedy actually takes place.

What these writers have contributed to fiction is broadly one thing: they have opened up for it a new area of life. They have added mental functioning and psychic existence to the already established domain of motive and action. They have created a fiction centered on the core of human experience, which if it has not been the usual domain of fiction, is not, they have proved, an improper one. Perhaps the most significant thing the stream-of-consciousness writers have demonstrated about the mind has been done obliquely: they have, through their contributions, proved that the human mind, especially the artist's, is too complex and wayward ever to be channeled into conventional patterns.

How these minds have been able to carry the awkward load of human consciousness into legitimate prose fiction is the concern of the rest of this study.

2

The Techniques

> *With their simple tools and primitive materials, it might be said, Fielding did well and Jane Austen even better, but compare their opportunities with ours!*
> VIRGINIA WOOLF

TECHNICAL EXPERIMENTATION has figured actively in the stream-of-consciousness novel. The satisfactory depiction of consciousness has required either the invention of new fictional techniques or a refocusing of the old ones. It is for this reason, doubtless, that the stream-of-consciousness *technique* is discussed in critical literature. This has unavoidably led to confusion, since the techniques for presenting stream of consciousness are greatly different from one novel to the next. It has led to the dilemma one has when one acknowledges that a particular piece of writing displays stream-of-consciousness technique and then turns to an entirely different kind of technique which has generally been labeled stream of consciousness also and sees no great similarity between the two. In this study, then, we shall be dealing with *techniques* and not with the stream-of-consciousness technique. In order to clarify the exposition, I shall avail myself of a simple classification to point to four basic techniques used in presenting stream of consciousness. They are direct interior monologue, indirect interior monologue, omniscient description, and soliloquy. There are, in addition, several special techniques with which a few writers have experimented.

Monologue intérieur is a term that is most often confused with stream of consciousness. It is used more accurately than the latter, since it is a rhetorical term and
properly refers to literary technique. But even this term
is in need of more precise definition, and it is greatly in
need of more limited application if it is to be a useful
critical term.

Édouard Dujardin, who claims to have used interior-
monologue technique first in his novel, *Les Lauriers sont
coupés* (1887), gave us what is unfortunately the standard definition of that technique as "the *speech* of a character in a scene, having for its object to introduce us
directly into the interior life of that character, *without
author intervention* through explanations or commentaries; . . . it differs from traditional monologue in that:
in its matter, it is an expression of the most *intimate
thought that lies nearest the unconscious;* in its form,
it is produced in direct phrases reduced to the minimum
of syntax; and thus it corresponds essentially to the
conception we have today of poetry."[1] The italics are
added and emphasize what is most confusing and finally
inaccurate about this definition. Rather than to continue
reliance on this as authority, it seems wise to use the
advantage of the passage of an important two decades
—important to the development of interior-monologue
techniques—to try a more simple and a more accurate
definition. Interior monologue is, then, the technique
used in fiction for representing the psychic content and
processes of character, partly or entirely unuttered, just
as these processes exist at various levels of conscious
control before they are formulated for deliberate speech.

Particularly, it should be noted that it is a technique of
representing psychic content and processes at various
levels of conscious control; that is, of representing consciousness. It should be emphasized that it may deal with
consciousness, however, at any level (it is not necessar-

ily, it is rarely, even, "an expression of the most intimate thought that lies nearest the unconscious"); and that it is concerned with the contents *and* the processes of consciousness, not with just one of these. It should be noted also that it is partly or entirely unuttered, for it represents the content of consciousness in its inchoate stage before it is formulated for deliberate speech. This is the differentia which separates interior monologue completely from dramatic monologue and stage soliloquy.

It is important to distinguish between two basic types of interior monologue, which can be conveniently designated as "direct" and "indirect." Direct interior monologue is that type of interior monologue which is represented with negligible author interference and with no auditor assumed. It is the type of monologue that Dujardin is concerned with in his definition. An examination of its special methods reveals: that it presents consciousness directly to the reader with negligible author interference; that is, there is either a complete or near-complete disappearance of the author from the page, with his guiding "he said"s and "he thought"s and with his explanatory comments. It should be emphasized that there is no auditor assumed; that is, the character is not speaking to anyone within the fictional scene; nor is the character speaking, in effect, to the reader (as the speaker of a stage monologue is, for example). In short the monologue is represented as being completely candid, as if there were no reader. This distinction is not easy to grasp, but it is a real one. Obviously, any author is writing, finally, for an audience. Even the Joyce of *Finnegans Wake* was. Joyce's audience is the abstracted reader who is given a private world, with no visible guide to direct him. The audience for the stage monologue likewise is being given a glimpse of privacy, but he has had charts and directions taught him previously in the form of well-established conventions. The result is that the stage monologue respects the audience's expectation of conventional syntax and diction and only *suggests* the possibilities of mental wandering; but the interior monologue proceeds in spite of the reader's expectations in order to represent the actual texture of consciousness—in order to represent it finally, however, *to the reader*.

Perhaps the most famous, and certainly the most extended and skillful direct interior monologue is that which comprises the last forty-five pages of James Joyce's *Ulysses*. It represents the meanderings of the consciousness of Molly Bloom while she is lying in bed. She has been awakened by the late arrival home of her wandering husband, with whom she has just conversed and who is lying asleep beside her. The opening few lines of the monologue will serve to recall its texture to the reader:

> Yes because he never did a thing like that before as ask to get his breakfast in bed with a couple of eggs since the *City Arms* hotel when he used to be pretending to be laid up with a sick voice doing his highness to made himself interesting to that old faggot Mrs. Riordan that he thought he had a great leg of and she never left us a farthing all for masses for herself and her soul greatest miser ever was actually afraid to lay out 4d for her methylated spirit telling me all her ailments. . . .[2]

There are two aspects of interior monologue in this passage to be considered: first, what there is about it to identify it as interior monologue; and second, what makes it *direct* interior monologue.

It will be remembered that these are not only the opening lines of this monologue, but that they are the opening lines of a section of the novel. There is no exposition preceding them. The situation will also be recalled: the character represented is alone except for her husband, who is asleep; hence, there is no auditor in the scene. The monologue is distinct from soliloquy because it is not presented, formally, for the information of the reader. The elements of incoherence and fluidity are emphasized by the complete absence of punctuation, of pronoun references, and of introductions to the persons and events Molly is thinking about, and by the frequent interruption of one idea by another. It is this incoherence and fluidity rather than what is specific as idea that is meant to be communicated. Here, the character is no more represented as speaking to the reader or even for his benefit than she is represented as speaking to another character in the scene. The monologue, rather, is interior; what is represented is the flow of Molly's consciousness. As the monologue progresses, it recedes to deeper levels of consciousness until Molly falls asleep, and the novel ends as the monologue ends.

In order to determine why this is *direct* interior monologue, this question must be asked: What role does the author play in the passage? As it is represented, he plays none. The author has disappeared entirely: it is in first person; the tense is, willy-nilly, past, imperfect, present, or conditional as Molly's mind dictates; and there are no commentaries, no stage directions from the author. Thus, this section of *Ulysses* dealing with Molly Bloom is, in its entirety, an example of sheer direct interior monologue. There are possibilities of variation, however.

The most frequent variation comes when the author intrudes as guide or commentator. Although this is common to the direct interior monologue, it is never more than slight, and it never goes so far that the monologue ceases to give the effect of being direct from the character. The appearance of the author is more frequent and necessary in monologues of psychologically complex characters, or in those which depict a deeper level of consciousness. Following is an example of this variation as it is handled by James Joyce in presenting, in *Ulysses*, Stephen Dedalus' consciousness:

> Woodshadows floated silently by through the morning peace from the stairhead seaward where

> he gazed. Inshore and farther out the mirror of wa-
> ter whitened, spurned by lightshod hurrying feet.
> *White breast of dim sea. The twining stresses, two
> by two. A hand plucking the harpstrings merging
> their twining chords. Wavewhite wedded words
> shimmering on the dim tide.* [P. 11.]

The asterisks are mine, and they enclose the direct monologue from Stephen's consciousness as I have interpreted the passage. The monologue continues for more
than a page until Stephen is interrupted in his reverie by
his friend, Buck Mulligan. During that monologue, the
author appears at two other points, each time more sub-
tly and less obviously than at the opening. It is notable
that the manner in which the author appears in this monologue is such that it would be scarcely perceptible to a
casual reader that he is there at all. The language of the
author fuses into the language of the character. Actually,
it is impossible, even after close analysis, to be certain
of the precise point at which the character's consciousness begins to be represented.

A very unusual use of the direct interior monologue
is that which attempts to depict dream consciousness (or
"unconsciousness," as one wishes). The only writers who
have attempted it in the novel are Joyce and Conrad
Aiken. Both of these writers base their depiction on psychoanalytical theories of dream mechanism. Significantly, and contrary to much opinion, the novels in
which this is done, such as *Finnegans Wake* and *The
Great Circle*, are the only ones in stream-of-consciousness literature in which there is a considerable Freudian
influence.[3]

Dujardin faces the problem of a kind of interior monologue that violates his definition because it uses the
third-person pronoun. He solves the problem by con-
cluding that third—and even second—person interior
monologue is merely disguise for first person. He does
this because of the analogy of interior monologue to con-

ventional discourse, with the possibilities in the latter of direct and indirect quotation; hence he uses the term here adopted of "indirect" interior monologue.[4]

From analysis of the technique, we find that Dujardin's term is useful, but only because of its general connotative advantages. It is true that one of the primary differences between direct and indirect interior monologue is the use of the first-person pronoun in the one, and third or second person in the other. But the third person is certainly not a "disguise" for the first person. The techniques are far different, both in the way they are manipulated and in their possible effects.

The basic difference between the two techniques is that indirect monologue gives to the reader a sense of the author's continuous presence; whereas direct monologue either completely or greatly excludes it. This difference in turn admits of special differences, such as the use of third-person instead of first-person point of view; the wider use of descriptive and expository methods to present the monologue; and the possibility of greater coherence and of greater surface unity through selection of materials. At the same time, the fluidity and sense of realism in the depiction of the states of consciousness can be maintained.

Indirect interior monologue is, then, that type of interior monologue in which an omniscient author presents unspoken material as if it were directly from the consciousness of a character and, with commentary and description, guides the reader through it. It differs from direct interior monologue basically in that the author intervenes between the character's psyche and the reader. The author is an on-the-scene guide for the reader. It retains the fundamental quality of interior monologue in that what it presents of consciousness is direct; that is, it is in the idiom and with the peculiarities of the character's psychic processes.

In practice, indirect interior monologue is usually combined with another of the techniques of stream of consciousness—especially with description of consciousness. Often, notably in Virginia Woolf's work, it is combined with direct monologue. This latter combination of techniques is especially suitable and natural, for the author who uses indirect monologue may see fit to drop out of the scene for a length of time, after he has introduced the reader to the character's mind with enough additional remarks for them to proceed smoothly together. Although it is Virginia Woolf among the stream-of-consciousness writers who relies most on the indirect interior monologue—and she uses it with great skill—it is to James Joyce again that we must go for an example because of his "pure" use of the technique. In the "Nausicaä" episode of *Ulysses,* that one which concerns the flirtation of Gerty MacDowell with Leopold Bloom, the reader enters the consciousness of Gerty, from whose point of view the episode is represented. Gerty is sitting on a rock near the seashore. Below her on the beach are her friends playing. Some distance away from her on the bridge is Leopold Bloom, watching her. Across the way an open-air dedicatory Mass is being celebrated:

> . . . Canon O'Hanlon handed the thurible back to Father Conroy and knelt down looking up at the Blessed Sacrament and the choir began to sing *Tantum ergo* and she [Gerty] just swung her foot in and out of time as the music rose and fell to the *Tantumer gosa cramen tum.* Three and eleven she paid for those stockings in Sparrow's of George's street on the Tuesday, no the Monday before Easter and there wasn't a brack on them and that was what he [Leopold] was looking at, transparent, and not at her [her friend, Cissy's] insignificant ones that had neither shape nor form (the cheek of her!) because he had eyes in his head to see the difference for himself. [P. 353.]

This passage, in context, is presented in the manner of straight narrative by the author; but it is distinguished by being in the fanciful, romantic idiom of the dreamy Gerty, and the material reflects the content of such a person's consciousness, especially its manner of associating. So what we have is, in effect, far more direct representation than mere description of Gerty's consciousness, for it is the mode of her consciousness that is represented. The consciousness is never presented directly, because the author is always present as the omniscient author with his comments. Through the device of a parody of sentimental fiction, the author gives an apparent interpretation, without any attempt to conceal himself from the reader, of Gerty's daydream consciousness.

For success in producing a more subtle effect through the use of this technique, we must look to Virginia Woolf, who uses it throughout two of her three novels that are most obviously concerned with stream of consciousness: *Mrs. Dalloway* and *To the Lighthouse*.

These novels contain a great deal of straight, conventional narration and description, but the interior monologue is used often enough to give the novels their special character of seeming to be always within the consciousness of the chief characters. Virginia Woolf says in her essay, "Modern Fiction": "Let us record the atoms as they fall upon the mind in the order in which they fall, let us trace the pattern, however disconnected and incoherent in appearances, which each sight or incident scores upon the consciousness." [5] And this is the best possible description of her method. Let us examine the opening lines of *Mrs. Dalloway:*

> Mrs. Dalloway said she would buy the flowers herself.
>
> For Lucy had her work cut out for her. The doors would be taken off their hinges; Rumpelmayer's men were coming. And then, thought Clarissa Dalloway, what a morning—fresh as if issued to children on a beach.
>
> What a lark! What a plunge! For so it has always

seemed to her, when, with a little squeak of the hinges, which she could hear now, she had burst open the French windows and plunged at Bourton into the open air. How fresh, how calm, stiller than this of course, the air was in the early morning; like the flap of a wave; the kiss of a wave, chill and sharp and yet (for a girl of eighteen as she then was) solemn, feeling as she did, standing there at the open window, that something awful was about to happen; looking at the flowers, at the trees with the smoke winding off them and the rooks rising, falling; standing and looking until Peter Walsh said, "Musing among the vegetables?"—was that it?—"I prefer men to cauliflowers"—was that it? He must have said it at breakfast one morning when she had gone out to the terrace—Peter Walsh. He would be back from India one of these days. . . .

If we compare this with the selection previously quoted from Molly Bloom's monologue, two things are immediately apparent as differences between them: first, the selection from Virginia Woolf is much more coherent than is the selection from Joyce; and second, the selection from Woolf is much more conventional in appearance than is the other. A slightly closer observation reveals two striking similarities that would distinguish either of these passages from ones taken from almost any other novels written before approximately 1915: There is in both of them, even in the Woolf passage, a studied element of incoherence; that is, references and meanings are intentionally vague and unexplained; and there is in both of them an element of disunity, of wandering from a single subject. The two similarities place both of the passages as possible excerpts from stream-of-consciousness novels; the two dissimilarities indicate they are different techniques within the stream-of-consciousness genre. When we turn to the second class of techniques, the more conventional ones, we discover that appearances are not always so obviously explanatory of method.

Conventional Modes

The second broad class of stream-of-consciousness techniques is not, like interior monologue, unique to the twentieth century in its fullest development. It is composed of standard and basic literary methods which writers of the stream-of-consciousness novel have put to special use. The most important of these methods are description by omniscient author and soliloquy.

The stream-of-consciousness technique that is most familiar to the reader of novels is description by an omniscient author. The basic convention which readers of fiction accept is the omniscience of the author. It has been so since fiction began, and seldom had the novelist been urged to disguise this fact until the late nineteenth century. From the time of the psychological novels of Dostoevski and Conrad, writers of fiction have realized the possibility for gaining greater verisimilitude, and hence reader-confidence, by altering the conventional focus of narration from the omniscient author to either the observer-author, the observer-character, the central character, or to some combination of these four possibilities.[6] It is something of a shock to realize that what is usually considered the most extreme form of the "experimental" novel is often worked out with the basic method of using conventional description by an omniscient author—without any attempt by the author to disguise the fact. The only thing unusual about it is the subject of this description, which, of course, in the stream-of-consciousness novel is the consciousness or psychic life of the characters.

This technique of stream of consciousness may be defined, simply, as the novelistic technique used for representing the psychic content and processes of a character in which an omniscient author describes that psyche through conventional methods of narration and description.[7] The technique is, in every case, combined with another of the basic techniques of stream of consciousness within any novel as a whole, although it is occasionally used alone in extended passages or in sections of a novel.

The novelist in English who uses this technique most consistently is Dorothy Richardson in the twelve volumes of *Pilgrimage*. Joyce, Faulkner, and Virginia Woolf all make use of it at one time or another. *Pilgrimage* is a representation of a portion of the adult life of one character, Miriam Henderson. The entire work is presented from the focal point of the omniscient author, but the omniscience is confined to Miriam's actions and thoughts. The effect is of a complete single point of view, Miriam's, although the method is conventional third-person description. This is possible because the author obviously identifies herself with her character. Such a technique is older than *Robinson Crusoe;* but the difference in Dorothy Richardson's work is that the life which she represents is largely the inner life of her character; that is, she represents Miriam's consciousness in its unformulated, unspoken, incoherent state. Only occasionally does the author leave ordinary descriptive methods to give the indirect interior monologue of her character. A selection from the second volume of *Pilgrimage* will illustrate this technique in its simplest form. Miriam and her mother are riding on a public, horse-drawn car, which has just been jolted by a bump in the street:

> The little shock sent her mind feeling out along the road they had just left. She considered its unbroken length, its shops, its treelessness. The wide thoroughfare, up which they now began to rumble, repeated it on a larger scale. The pavements were wide causeways reached from the roadway by stone steps, three deep. The people passing along them were unlike any she knew. They were all alike. They were . . . She could find no word for the

strange impression they made. It coloured the whole of the district through which they had come. It was part of the new world to which she was pledged to go on September 18th. It was her world already, and she had no words for it. She would not be able to convey it to others. She felt sure her mother had not noticed it. She must deal with it alone. To try to speak about it, even with Eve, would sap her courage. It was her secret. A strange secret for all her life as Hanover had been. But Hanover was beautiful. . . .[8]

Two things are notable in this passage: first, that the reader is always within the mind of the character, Miriam; and second, that the method is entirely descriptive, and it is written in the third person. It remains necessary only to distinguish this technique from indirect interior monologue in order to establish it as one of the basic techniques of the stream-of-consciousness novel.

The distinction is implicit in the definitions of the two techniques, especially in that part of the definition of indirect interior monologue which states that "an omniscient author presents unspoken material directly from the psyche." This is the fundamental difference between the two techniques, and it is a difference that separates them widely and that changes their respective possible effects, textures, and scopes. The use of description by an omniscient author to represent consciousness allows for almost as many variations as there are of style in general. There is one technique, however, the soliloquy, which is even more flexible in other directions.

The soliloquy differs from the interior monologue primarily in that, although it is spoken *solus*, it nevertheless is represented with the assumption of a formal and immediate audience. This, in turn, gives it special characteristics which distinguish it from internal monologue. The most important of these is a greater coherence, since the purpose of it is to communicate emotions and ideas which are related to a plot and action; whereas the purpose of interior monologue is, first of all, to communicate psychic identity. Novelists who are concerned with the stream-of-consciousness genre have found the soliloquy a useful device for depicting consciousness.

Soliloquy in the stream-of-consciousness novel may be defined as the technique of representing the psychic content and processes of a character directly from character to reader without the presence of an author, but with an audience tacitly assumed. Hence, it is less candid, necessarily, and more limited in the depth of consciousness that it can represent than is interior monologue. The point of view is always the character's, and the level of consciousness is usually close to the surface. In practice, the purpose of the stream-of-consciousness novel which employs soliloquy is achieved occasionally by the combination of soliloquy with interior monologue.

There are several highly successful novels in English which use the soliloquy to depict the stream of consciousness. One of these, William Faulkner's *As I Lay Dying,* is composed entirely of the soliloquies of fifteen characters. The plot is reduced to a minimum of complexity: It concerns the preparations for a dying woman's burial and the attempts to get her buried after she is dead. Most of the characters are members of her family. Sometimes they reflect only the surface attitudes they have toward the proceedings; at other times there is a complex attitude expressed which reveals more of the workings of the whole consciousness. Obviously this novel is greatly concerned with those attitudes that lie on the threshold of consciousness. A single excerpt from it will not reveal the stream-of-consciousness quality of the whole, but it will allow us to examine the details of the technique. The person speaking is Jewel, one of the dying woman's sons; he is stimulated by the sight of his brother, Cash, making the coffin under the mother's death-room window:

It's because he stays out there, right under the window, hammering and sawing on that goddamn box. Where she's got to see him. Where every breath she draws is full of his knocking and sawing where she can see him saying See. See what a good one I am making for you. I told him to go somewhere else. I said Good God do you want to see her in it. It's like when he was a little boy and she says if she had some fertilizer she would try to raise some flowers and he taken the bread-pan and brought it back from the barn full of dung.[9]

According to the explanation above concerning the manner in which soliloquy is used as a stream-of-consciousness technique, it is not surprising to find this passage more coherent than have been the passages of interior monologue we have examined. But even here there are some unmistakable signs of stream of consciousness which one would not find in conventional soliloquy. It is particularly noticeable in the sentence structure. Allowing for the idiom of the character, there remains an arrangement of thought units *as they would originate in the character's consciousness,* rather than as they would be deliberately expressed. Such a fragment as "where she's got to see him" indicates the thought as it arrives, just as does such a sentence as the following: "It's like when he was a little boy and she says if she had some fertilizer she would try to raise some flowers and he taken the bread-pan and brought it back from the barn full of dung." This latter sentence, with its three independent clauses and its metaphorical complexity and subtlety, represents one image, the image which in Jewel's consciousness preceded the verbalization of it.

The use of soliloquy as a stream-of-consciousness technique has a special significance. It should be noted that the dates of the outstanding novels in English which use this technique (*As I Lay Dying* [1930] and Virginia Woolf's *The Waves* [1931]) are relatively late, about fifteen years after Joyce, Richardson, and Woolf published their first works which adumbrated stream of consciousness in the novel. The techniques for presenting stream of consciousness had developed much in those fifteen years. This development was partly from the stimulus of growing interest in psychoanalysis, partly from the masterful display of technique in *Ulysses,* and greatly from the emergence of novelists who recognized the value of depicting prespeech consciousness, but who wanted also to utilize the advantages of the traditional novel of plot and action. These novels using soliloquy represent a successful combination of interior stream of consciousness with exterior action. In other words, both internal and external character is depicted in them. The method for achieving this could not have been interior monologue, for greater coherence and more unity were needed than that technique provides; nor did simple description prove sufficiently variable. It was the soliloquy which was found flexible enough to carry the double load.

The inevitable experimenting within the stream-of-consciousness genre has led to the development of a number of special techniques. Two of these are particularly interesting, and a brief consideration of them will be informative in relation to the whole study. These are drama and verse form. The qualities that make these techniques "special" are their uniqueness and their relative lack of service so far as the whole genre is concerned.

Only in one instance, so far as I can determine, is actual dramatic technique used to present stream of consciousness in fiction. That is in the work of the great artificer, James Joyce. The climactic episode of *Ulysses* is the fifteenth one, the one which corresponds to the "Circe" episode of the *Odyssey.* It is presented in the form of a theatrical scene, with characters and dialogue, acting directions, costume descriptions, entrances, etc. So far as the surface level of the novel is concerned, this episode takes place in "Night-town" in Dublin, chiefly in a brothel, at about midnight. The principal characters of the episode are Leopold, Stephen, the whore-mistress Bella, and one of her girls named Zoe. The remarkable thing, however, for this discussion is the actual setting of the scene, which is the minds of Stephen and Bloom. The significant action takes place on a hallucinatory level, and it is a fantasy; or more specifically, it is an objectified representation of the minds of Leopold and Stephen while those persons are in a state of hysteria caused by fatigue and too much alcohol. This results in mild hallucinations for both of them, so that there are dozens of characters involved, including almost all of the persons Leopold and Stephen have seen or thought about during the day, living or dead; and as if this were not enough, most of the inanimate objects which have been prominent in the lives and minds of the two characters are personified here.

What is accomplished by the use of drama techniques in this stream-of-consciousness novel is the objective representation of the unspoken mental life of the two chief characters while they are in a condition which makes their mental processes even more chaotic and fluid than they ordinarily are. At the same time, on other thematic levels, other things are achieved (such as the integrating of motifs and the elaboration of the burlesque epic pattern) simply because of the increased free play of the psychic processes. As Harry Levin comments, "Joyce, by this time has set going enough trains of thought and accumulated enough contexts of experience to externalize his internal dialogue before the footlights of consciousness."[10]

The attempt to represent especially chaotic mental states accounts also for another special technique. Unfortunately for the novels of Waldo Frank, the one writer who employs this method considerably, this technique lacks the objectifying virtue which makes dramatic technique successful.

Although verse quotations, usually in the form of incomplete snatches of either doggerel or great poetry, are used within one or another of the basic techniques by both Joyce and Virginia Woolf, the only novel which actually contains verse form to present psychic content is Waldo Frank's *Rahab*. This novel is not important enough for us to consider at length; however, the use of verse in this manner is an interesting experiment and it should be pointed out. According to Joseph Warren Beach, Frank uses verse when he wants to present the materials of consciousness as being highly emotional.[11] This is a euphemistic way of saying Frank presents consciousness in verse form when he has no specific "objective correlative" to convey the emotional complexion of a character. This is a situation which seldom exists for the more responsible writers.

One example of this technique will suffice to show the method and its obvious shortcomings in actually representing psychic states. Clara, one of the minor characters, is "thinking" of how happy she is that Fanny Luve, the protagonist, is still living with her:

> —You are not well yet, you are not
> ready to leave me.
> What is the matter with you?
> Why are you still here?
> O I am glad you are here! You
> are balm, you are pressing
> sharpness on my ache. .
> I do not understand.[12]

The inchoate aspect of nonverbalized emotion is the only thing communicated by this verse. Waldo Frank has set himself an impossible task in trying to depict consciousness in verse form. There are two important aspects of psychic processes which are opposed by two inherent aspects of verse: first, the psyche is characterized by being logically unordered; whereas verse suggests a specific form of logical ordering; and second, psychic processes are further characterized by their unstable focusing powers; whereas verse, when it approaches the status of lyrical poetry as Frank's does, tends to center on one subject. This technique, then, is far less effective in presenting stream of consciousness than are the basic techniques.

Direct and indirect interior monologue, omniscient description, and prose soliloquy have proved to be, in the hands of the most skillful writers, capable of carrying the strange and awkward load of human consciousness into the realms of legitimate prose fiction. There have been difficulties along the way, however, which have demanded application of many invented and borrowed techniques in order for them to be overcome. Most of these difficulties were owing to the nature of the load itself. The remaining pages of this study will be devoted to an explanation of the problems and a consideration of how they were overcome. Or, to leave the metaphor, we shall, next, investigate the methods stream-of-consciousness writers have used to capture and control, for fictional purposes, the fundamental nature of consciousness.

The Stream

Despite their great differences in handling basic methods, writers of stream-of-consciousness fiction have found a common necessity shaping the minutiae of their techniques. This necessity has its source in the nature of any fundamental concept of consciousness and in the basic problems of representing it within the limitations of coherent fiction.

Every responsible writer is sufficiently disillusioned about his medium to realize that there are technical limitations past which he cannot go. Even such a virtuoso as James Joyce never believed that he could actually present the consciousness of a character with exactness. Here, our analysis is to determine the possible technical devices by which consciousness can be represented convincingly and to determine the controls by

41

which selection of materials can be made. But the problem must be stated more concretely before the analysis can be meaningful.

What, then, are the essential problems of depicting consciousness in fiction? There are two orders of them and both come from the nature of consciousness itself. First, a particular consciousness, we assume, is a private thing; and second, consciousness is never static but is always in a state of motion. The first of these is dependent on the second, so we shall occupy ourselves now with the problem of the flux of consciousness.

Complex theory need not concern us in order to determine the nature of the movement of consciousness, since what is obvious is enough to set up difficult problems for any writer. Consciousness, first of all, is considered in its movement fluid and unbound by arbitrary time concepts by these writers who belong to the generation following William James and Henri Bergson. "Fluid" does not mean a smooth flow necessarily. The flow of consciousness, it might be admitted, is found on levels nearing the state of unconsciousness, but as the prespeech levels nearer the surface are the subject of most stream-of-consciousness fiction, the checks and interferences to the flow from the outer world become an important consideration. In short, the term "stream" is not fully descriptive. The notion of synthesis must be added to that of flux to indicate the quality of being sustained, of being able to absorb interferences after the flow is momentarily broken, and of being able to pass freely from one level of consciousness to another. The other important characteristic of the movement of consciousness is its ability to move freely in time—its tendency to find its own time sense. The premise is that the psychic processes, before they are rationally controlled for communication purposes, do not follow a calendar continuity. Everything that enters consciousness is there at the "present moment"; furthermore, the event of this "moment," no matter how much clock time it occupies, may be infinitely extended by being broken up into its parts, or it may be highly compressed into a flash of recognition. With this skeletal concept of the nature of the movement of consciousness, let us see how the quality is rendered into fictional form.

The chief technique in controlling the movement of stream of consciousness in fiction has been an application of the principles of psychological free association. The primary facts of free association are the same whether they are suspended in the psychology of Locke-Hartley or of Freud-Jung; and they are simple. The psyche, which is almost continuously active, cannot be concentrated for very long in its processes, even when it is most strongly willed; when little effort is exerted to concentrate it, its focus remains on any one thing but momentarily. Yet the activity of consciousness must have content, and this is provided for by the power of one thing to suggest another through an association of qualities in common or in contrast, wholly, or partially—even to the barest suggestion. Three factors control the association: first, the memory, which is its basis; second, the senses, which guide it; and third, the imagination, which determines its elasticity. The subtlety of play, the rank of precedence and the physiology of these factors are problems of dispute among psychologists. None of the stream-of-consciousness writers, except to a limited extent Joyce in *Finnegans Wake* and Conrad Aiken, has been concerned with the complexities of the psychological problems; but all of the writers have recognized the primacy of free association in determining the movement of the psychic processes of their characters.[13]

The importance of free association and the skill with which it can be used to represent the quality of movement in the psychic processes is most clearly represented by the interior monologue technique in Joyce's work. The elemental content of Molly Bloom's psyche lends itself to informative analysis. In the following excerpt,

the monologue is nearing completion and Molly is trying
to go to sleep. The predominant motif in her consciousness is a reawakening of an emotional interest in her
husband, who is lying beside her asleep. The reader will
remember that the entire monologue of forty-five pages
is presented without a break; consequently, the excerpt
begins in the middle of a line of type. The exegetical
comments within the parentheses are intended to point
up the association process:

. . . *quarter after* (a clock nearby has impinged on
Molly's consciousness to remind her of the time) *what
an unearthly hour I suppose theyre just getting up in
China now combing out their pigtails for the day* (her
imagination has slipped off to China, still under the
stimulus of the striking clock) *well soon have the nuns
ringing the angelus* (she is still concerned about how
late it is) *theyve nobody coming in to spoil their sleep*
(as Leopold did hers) *except an odd priest or two for his
night office* (her attention has slipped back to her husband's late arrival home, which is the reason she is now
awake; but the time is still predominant in her consciousness) *the alarmclock next door at cockshout clattering
the brains out of itself* (she anticipates an annoying
occurrence of the mornings and again becomes anxious
about losing sleep) *let me see if I can doze off 1 2 3 4 5*
(the anticipation of the neighbor's early alarm stimulates her to exert her will, and she tries to count herself
to sleep) *what kind of flowers are those they invented
like the stars* (in trying to focus her attention she has
noticed the flowers on the wallpaper and then she tries
to remember the name of a particular flower) *the wallpaper in Lombard street was much nicer* (her attention
is now to the wallpaper at a former dwelling) *the apron
he gave me was like that* (the "he" refers again to her
husband, and she remembers an apron he gave her—evidently with flowers on it similar to the ones on her present wallpaper) *something only* (that is, only something

44

like it; the resemblance is vague, but enough to asso-
ciate it with her husband, who probably gave it to her
when they lived on Lombard street) *I only wore it
twice* (the apron still) *better lower this lamp and try
again so as I can get up early* (she is anxious still about
the lateness, but she is also reminded by the apron her
husband gave her that he has ordered her to serve him
breakfast in bed—hence she will have to get up early—
and that he had brought home with him Stephen Dedalus, who represents refinement and youth to Molly) *Ill
go to Lambes there beside Findlaters and get them to
send us some flowers to put about the place in case he
brings him home tomorrow* (the flower motif reënters
while she meditates an imagined reception of Stephen)
today I mean (again the lateness) *no no Fridays an un-
lucky day* (superstition somewhere in her consciousness
does not want to acknowledge Friday as the day) *first I
want to do the place up somewhat* (back to her plans for
entertaining Stephen) *the dust grows in it I think while
Im asleep* (she is concerned about the tidiness of her
house and perhaps indirectly again about not sleeping)
*then we can have music and cigarettes I can accompany
him* (again she imagines a day with Stephen) *first I
must clean the keys of the piano with milk whatll I wear
shall I wear a white rose* (she considers her impression
on Stephen and thinks again of a flower) *or those fairy
cakes in Liptons* (her attention focuses on her projected
shopping tour in the morning) *I love the smell of a rich
big shop at 7 1/2d. a lb or the other ones with the cherries
in them and the pinky sugar 11d a couple of lbs* (she contemplates the sensations of being in the shop, and then
of actually making purchases) *of course a nice plant for
the middle of the table* (back to flowers and plans for
entertaining Stephen) *Id get that cheaper in wait
wheres this I saw them not long ago* (she thinks of another shop the name of which she can't quite remember)
*I love flowers Id love to have the whole place swimming
in roses* (the renewed idea of a flower shop stimulates

her imagination) *God of heaven theres nothing like nature* (from flowers to nature in general) *the wild mountains then the sea and the waves rushing then the beautiful country with fields of oats and wheat and all kinds of things . . . and lakes and flowers all sorts of shapes and smells . . . primroses and violets nature it is* (with a rush of images she defines her connotations of nature) *as for them saying theres no God I wouldnt give a snap of my two fingers for all their learning* (her love for nature puts her in an aggressively proreligious frame of mind—further down in her consciousness she probably is attacking Stephen's intellectuality).

Molly thinks about "atheists" further: she thinks that "they might as well try to stop the sun from rising"; this reminds her of Leopold's comment that "the sun shines for you," which he said during their courtship; she contemplates this event further and is reminded of details of the days she lived in Gibraltar where the courtship occurred; finally, she returns to Leopold's conquest (all amid flowers) and the monologue ends: ". . . and how he kissed me under the Moorish wall and I thought well as well him as another and then I asked him with my eyes to ask again yes and then asked me would I yes to say yes my mountain flower and first I put my arms around him yes and drew him down to me so he could feel my breasts all perfume yes and his heart was going like mad and yes I said yes I will Yes." The ending is a fade-out as Molly finally goes to sleep with Leopold receiving her capital affirmation.

In skeleton outline the movement of Molly's stream of consciousness, as it is controlled by the principle of free association through memory, the senses, and the imagination, is clear:

Hears clock
1) *imagines* Chinese arising
2) *anticipates* (memory) the Angelus
   3) *imagines* nuns' sleep

46

4) *anticipates* next-door alarm
("Alarm" stimulates her to attempt control of consciousness; counts)

Sees wallpaper
  5) *remembers* star-shaped flowers
  6) *remembers* Lombard street dwelling
  7) *remembers* apron Leopold gave her
(Thought of Leopold; attempts to control consciousness)

Lowers lamp
  8) *reminded* has to get up early
  9) *imagines* the next day
    10) *imagines* shopping
      11) *imagines* bake shop
      12) *imagines* making purchases
    13) *imagines* receiving Dedalus
      14) *anticipates* cleaning house
      15) *imagines* entertainment for Dedalus
      16) *anticipates* cleaning piano keys
      17) *imagines* her attire
      18) *imagines* flowers for the table
        19) *imagines* room swimming in roses
          20) *contemplates* (memory and imagination) "nature"
            21) *sees* (imagination) panorama of nature
              22) *imagines* argument she would give atheist: "may as well stop the sun"
                23) *recalls* statement of Leopold's about the sun during courtship
                  24) *recalls* scene of courtship
                    25) *recalls* details of Gibraltar
                      26) *recalls* details of courting
                        27) fade-out.

The very pattern of the outline itself shows the direction of Molly's stream. The hearing of the clock, the seeing of the wallpaper, and the lowering of the lamp indicate places where the outer world impinges on Molly's inner life. After the last of these, the line of thought goes steadily away from the outer world as Molly falls asleep. Each detail is, it will be noted, carefully associated with a previous one.

All stream-of-consciousness fiction is greatly dependent on the principles of free association. This is true of such different-textured techniques as direct interior monologue and simple omniscient description of consciousness. The main difference in the manner in which free association is employed in these diverse techniques is the frequency with which it is used. A second difference is in the subtlety and complexity with which it is used.

Take, for example, two extremes of stream-of-consciousness technique: On the side of the complex there is the attempt by Joyce in *Finnegans Wake* to present dream consciousness; and on the side of the simple there is Dorothy Richardson's impressionistic depiction of consciousness in *Pilgrimage*. Both writers rely on free association to give direction to the materials of consciousness. In *Finnegans Wake* the principle can be seen operating almost from word to word and distressingly often between syllables within a single word. When Joyce uses such a "word" as *expolodotonotes,* it is at least partly because *detonate* was associated with *explode.* When he uses *umbrilla-parasoul* the associations are so numerous, so complex, so erudite, and on so many levels that one critic has used fifty lines of small type to point them out.[14] The comments here are not meant to be deprecatory; they are meant to indicate that here is the principle of free association to determine microscopically the movement of H. C. Earwicker's dream.

At the other extreme is Dorothy Richardson's description of her character's consciousness. Free association is employed distinctly, but infrequently, in *Pilgrimage.* Although the process is fairly obvious there, the author boldly explains it in such phrases as, "The little shock sent her mind feeling out"; or she uses simple conjunctions to indicate the association, such as, "A strange secret for all her life as Hanover had been. *But* [my italics] Hanover was beautiful. . . ." The point is, whatever the texture, whatever the depth, it is the process of psychological free association which is used by stream-of-consciousness writers to guide the direction of their characters' streams.

Time- and Space-Montage

Another set of devices for controlling the movement of stream-of-consciousness fiction is a group that may be analogically termed "cinematic" devices. The interplay between the motion picture and fiction in the twentieth century provides material for an enlightening and enormously valuable study. Here we can examine only one small facet of it.[15]

A basic device for the cinema is that of montage. Among the secondary devices are such controls as "multiple-view," "slow-ups," "fade-outs," "cutting," "close-ups," "panorama," and "flash-backs." "Montage" in the film sense refers to a class of devices which are used to show interrelation or association of ideas, such as a rapid succession of images or the superimposition of image on image or the surrounding of a focal image by related ones. It is essentially a method to show composite or diverse views of one subject—in short, to show multiplicity. The secondary techniques are methods for achieving the effect of montage; devices for overcoming the two-dimensional limitation of the screen. Some of them are concerned with achieving the flow of events; others, such as the "slow-up," "close-up," and sometimes the "fade-out," are more concerned with subjective details, or as Professor Beach has said, with "the infinite expansion of the moment." The thing about this that is most pertinent to using the analogy for fiction technique is that montage and the secondary devices have to do with transcending or modifying arbitrary and conventional time and space barriers.

There are, then, devices analogous to these in stream-of-consciousness fiction to which the same terms are applied. David Daiches, who does not use the terms of the analogy, explains the method very well as it is used in Virginia Woolf's novels, although it is James Joyce who is most frequently noticed as the brilliant exponent of the device. Both Joyce and Woolf use it, as do other stream-of-consciousness writers, because the quality of consciousness itself demands a movement that is not rigid clock progression. It demands instead the freedom of shifting back and forth, of intermingling past, present, and imagined future. In representing this montage in fiction, Daiches points out there are two methods: one is that in which the subject can remain fixed in space and his consciousness can move in time—the result is time-montage or the superimposition of images or ideas from one time on those of another; the other possibility, of course, is for time to remain fixed and for the spatial element to change, which results in space-montage.[16] This latter method does not necessarily involve the representation of consciousness, although it is used frequently as an auxiliary technique in stream-of-consciousness fiction. It is referred to variously as the "camera eye" or as "multiple view"—terms which suggest the possibility of the concurrence of plural images at one point in time.

The chief function of all of the cinematic devices, particularly of the basic one of montage, is to express movement and coexistence. It is this ready-made device for representing the nonstatic and the nonfocused which the stream-of-consciousness writers have grasped to aid them in accomplishing what is, after all, their fundamental purpose: to represent the dual aspect of human life—the inner life simultaneously with the outer life.

A look at Virginia Woolf's artistry will suggest how the cinematic method is transferred to fiction. In the opening pages of *Mrs. Dalloway,* the basic method of indirect interior monologue is used to present Clarissa Dalloway to the reader. We stay within Clarissa's consciousness for the first sixteen pages (Modern Library Edition), except for a few brief paragraphs. Thus the spatial relationship is static (although Clarissa is leisurely walking along in London). The number of images, however, is amazing, as is their diversity in subject and in time of occurrence. A summary record of them for only several pages reveals a fairly complex montage effect with most of the cinematic devices being used. The following outline synopsis records only the major images, which are sufficient to illustrate the principle of montage. The unifying subject, as it is in almost all stream-of-consciousness passages, is the character's egocentric consciousness:

First, Clarissa thinks of preparations for a party in the immediate future; then she shifts to the present moment and considers what a fine morning it is; there is a "flashback" over twenty years in which she thinks of the fine days at Bourton (the principle of free association is working here also, of course); still in the past, but on a specific day she recalls a conversation with Peter Walsh in minute detail (the "close-up" in operation); there follows a vision in the near future of Peter Walsh's proposed visit to London; at this point, the device of "multiple-view" is employed and we leave Clarissa's consciousness for a few lines to enter that of a stranger who observes Clarissa crossing the street; back in Clarissa's stream, we find her contemplating, in the present moment, her love for Westminster; there is a "fade-out" of her sentimental musings and she recalls the previous evening's conversation about the War being over; this in turn "fades-out" and we are back with her joy at being part of London at the present moment; here the principle of "cutting" is employed to present a brief conversation Clarissa has with Hugh Whitbread, whom she meets on the street;

the conversation, as it is freely reported, "fades-out" to lose itself in Clarissa's stream of consciousness again while she is concerned with various aspects of the Whitbreads; the time quickly shifts (with images of the Whitbreads) from an indefinite past, to the present moment, to the immediate future, and to the far past; still in the far past, Clarissa thinks of Peter and Hugh at Bourton; this is abruptly changed by "cutting" to contemplations again of the fine weather at the present moment; which "fades-out" to thoughts of Clarissa's own "divine vitality" as she knew herself in the indefinite past.

The record to now has covered only six of the first unit of sixteen pages, but this is sufficient to illustrate the time-montage of Clarissa's consciousness, and how it, along with free association, defines the movement of the stream.

Movement of consciousness analogous to the cinematic device of montage is more easily illustrated in indirect interior monologue (which the passage just dealt with is) than it is with a passage of direct monologue, such as the one previously examined from Molly Bloom's episode in *Ulysses*. If Molly's entire monologue were considered, the device of montage would be equally apparent; but any one, even lengthy, passage is composed so much of subjective detail (with the cinematic devices of "slow-up" and "close-up" at work) that the broad movement is scarcely discernible.

For the other method of montage, that in which the time element is static and the space element moves, it is Joyce who has elicited praise from the famous exponent of montage in the films, Sergei Eisenstein.[17] In the "Wandering Rocks" episode of *Ulysses* especially, Joyce has exploited this device. It ought to be stated that whereas Joyce is the great virtuoso of the technique, it is Virginia Woolf in *Mrs. Dalloway* and in *To the Lighthouse* who blends it most expertly and effectively with other stream-of-consciousness techniques. Joyce utilizes space-montage as his basic technique and superimposes interior monologue on it; Virginia Woolf maintains her basic interior monologue method and superimposes montage on it.

The tenth, or "Wandering Rocks," episode in *Ulysses* consists of eighteen scenes taking place in various parts of Dublin. Joyce is careful to make cross references of minor details to indicate that the scenes take place at approximately the same time. Except for these minor and superficial details the scenes are unrelated. Stuart Gilbert calls this the "labyrinth" technique.[18] It is a superb example of space-montage. Many of the scenes employ one or another of the stream-of-consciousness techniques, but it is only in those scenes which concern Leopold Bloom and Stephen Dedalus that the stream-of-consciousness function of the novel is carried on. The remaining scenes of the episode, which form its greater part, cause it to be one of the several panoramic parts of *Ulysses.* Insofar as this episode does concern the psychic processes of the two main characters, however, it illustrates the function of space-montage as a control of the movement of the stream of consciousness. Its advantage is in the aesthetic justification it establishes for presenting brief and random glimpses into consciousness.

For example, in one of the scenes of the episode, Leopold Bloom is presented as looking at mildly pornographic literature in a bookshop in order to find a novel to present to his wife. We get this glimpse into his unuttered thoughts:

> Mr. Bloom, alone, looked at the titles. *Fair Tyrants* by James Lovebirch. Know the kind that is. Had it? Yes.
>
> He opened it. Thought so.
>
> A woman's voice behind the dingy curtain. Listen: The man.
>
> No: she wouldn't like that much. Got her it once.

He read the other title: *Sweets of Sin.* More in her line. Let us see.

He read where his finger opened.

—*All the dollarbills her husband gave her were spent in the stores on wondrous gowns and costliest frillies. For him! For Raoul!*

Yes. This. Here. Try.

—*Her mouth glued on his in a luscious voluptuous kiss while his hands felt for the opulent curves inside her deshabille.*

Yes. Take this. The end. [P. 232.]

This scene is "cut" after a few more lines and shifts to an auction in another part of Dublin. The secondary cinematic device which comes to greatest use in this episode is that of "cutting." The actual substance of Bloom's monologue here has no relationship to the rest of the "Wandering Rocks" episode, except possibly to the scene where Stephen Dedalus is also depicted as buying books. This "camera eye" method of presenting stream of consciousness enables Joyce to give the reader a glimpse into a single aspect of Bloom's psyche. It is an aspect which needs only a few lines to present and which would defeat its function if it were elaborated on. It also enables Joyce to do something more important: It explains to the reader images and phrases which constantly crop up in Bloom's monologue throughout the remaining part of the day; for Raoul's bold romance in the *Sweets of Sin* haunts and tempts and even becomes a symbol for poor cuckolded Leopold Bloom. Richard Kain in his compilation of word motifs in *Ulysses* has, in fact, shown that the name "Raoul," for example, appears in Bloom's monologues seven times after his initial reading of it at the bookshop, and "sweets of sin" appears thirteen times.[19]

Despite the admirable way in which all this is done, it is Virginia Woolf who uses the device of space-montage most effectively so far as the purposes of stream-of-consciousness fiction are concerned. This is because she manages to relate it to her other characteristic devices and to subordinate it to her basic stream-of-consciousness subject matter. Perhaps the most frequently cited example of multiple-view, or space-montage, in recent fiction is the scene in *Mrs. Dalloway* in which the airplane is skywriting. Let us see how that scene is worked into the stream-of-consciousness bias of the novel.

> Suddenly Mrs. Coates [one of a group watching at the gates of Buckingham Palace] looked up into the sky. The sound of an aeroplane bored ominously into the ears of the crowd. There it was coming over the trees, letting out white smoke from behind, which curled and twisted, actually writing something! making letters in the sky! every one looked up.
>
> . . . .
>
> "Glaxo," said Mrs. Coates in a strained, awe-stricken voice . . .
>
> "Kreemo," murmured Mrs. Bletchley, like a sleepwalker. With his hat held out perfectly still in his hand, Mr. Bowley gazed straight up. . . .
>
> The aeroplane turned and raced and swooped exactly where it liked, swiftly, freely, like a skater—
>
> "That's an E," said Mrs. Bletchley—or a dancer—
>
> "It's toffee," murmured Mr. Bowley—
>
> It had gone; it was behind the clouds. . . . Then suddenly, as a train comes out of a tunnel, the aeroplane rushed out of the clouds again, the sound boring into the ears of all the people in the Mall, in the Green Park, in Piccadilly, in Regent Street, in Regent's Park. . . .
>
> Lucrezia Warren Smith, sitting by her husband's side on a seat in Regent's Park in the Broad Walk, looked up.

"Look, look, Septimus!" she cried. . . .

So, thought Septimus, looking up, they are sig-
nalling to me. Not indeed in actual words. . . .

There follow several pages of Septimus' interior monologue, occasionally interrupted by his awareness of the
airplane. Then, we are brought back to Clarissa Dalloway, whom we had left at the beginning of the montage
section, just as she arrives back home asking the maid,
"What are they looking at?" This is a reference, of course,
to the spectacle of the plane.[20]

What Virginia Woolf has done for her reader by the
use of montage here is not only to give him a cross-
section view of London as it responds to the same
stimulus which her two chief characters, Clarissa and
Septimus, receive (which in itself is important for understanding their psyches), but she accomplishes other
purposes: mainly, she introduces us to Septimus' psyche
in its only overt relationship possible to that of her protagonist—that is, its relation in time and space. To appreciate this, it must be remembered that the linking of
Septimus and Clarissa, whose relationship is tenuous
and who never meet, has a profound significance symbolically. Another purpose that is accomplished is the
unified introduction of Septimus into Clarissa's story,
especially the sharp shifting and the quick cutting of his
monologue in order to trace anew the movement of
Clarissa's consciousness. It can be seen readily that once
the roving camera is accepted, the seemingly arbitrary
choosing of subject after subject is acceptable. So one is
not shocked by the sudden inclusion or the sudden cutting off of anything. The object of central focus in the
montage, in this instance the skywriting plane, carries
the burden of unity. James Joyce, the other employer of
montage, is seldom so considerate, for, as we shall see,
his unifying devices are usually external rather than organic: For Joyce, one must be well-informed as well as
sensitive.

A Note on Mechanics

Another set of controls is of less importance than free association and the cinematic devices, but it is necessary to consider these controls if we are to understand how the quality of movement of consciousness is represented in fiction. This set comprises the mechanical devices. It has been pointed out earlier that typographical and punctuation controls serve to give the effect of directness to interior monologue, and that, at the same time, they allow the author on-the-scene control of the monologue. Their function in controlling the movement of stream of consciousness is similar, but more complex. These devices, although they are usually functional for every reader, when they are used in stream-of-consciousness fiction ought to be considered with special care. They are often signals for important changes in direction, pace, time, or even in character focus; occasionally they are the only indications of such changes. A few illustrations will show the important function of these mechanics—and the ingenuity with which they are handled—in controlling the movement of consciousness.

The most organic use of punctuation to control movement of stream of consciousness is that of William Faulkner in *The Sound and the Fury.* In this novel direct interior monologue is always indicated at its beginning by italics. The italics have a further function: they signal to the reader that there is a shift in time. It is a shift which is usually sudden. Unless the reader is aware of this important function of the italics, he is likely to be confused. One illustration will suffice. Benjy, the idiot, is being guided along a fence overlooking a golf course by Luster, his keeper. The excerpt begins with Luster speaking aloud to Benjy.

> "You snagged on that nail again. Cant you never crawl through here without snagging on that nail."

> *Caddy uncaught me and we crawled through.*
> *Uncle Maury said to not let anybody see us, so we*
> *better stoop over, Caddy said. Stoop over, Benjy.*
> *Like this, see. We stooped over and crossed the*
> *garden, where the flowers rasped and rattled*
> *against us. The ground was hard. . . .*
>
> *Keep your hands in your pockets, Caddy said. Or*
> *they'll get froze. You dont want your hands froze*
> *on Christmas, do you.*
>
> "It's too cold out there." Versh said. "You dont
> want to go out of doors."
>
> "What is it now." Mother said.[21]

What has happened is that Benjy's snagging himself reminds him of another time eighteen years before when he snagged himself while he was with his sister, Caddy. This memory is presented in the italics. However, the resumption of straight dialogue after the italicized section does not represent a continuation of the dialogue that had preceded the italics; it is a continuation of Benjy's stream of memory of the past. When italics do appear again (two pages later), they indicate a shift of time to the present.

Although other writers have not found the use of italics necessary to maintain fluidity in the depiction of consciousness, seldom have other writers been able to disappear from their narrative as completely as Faulkner does here. They have, however, used other devices of punctuation. Virginia Woolf's reliance on punctuation to control the representation of consciousness movement is limited to the use of parentheses. She uses them sparingly and effectively; she does not rely on them as a consistent signal as Faulkner does with italics. A few lines from *To the Lighthouse* will indicate her method. We are, so to speak, with Mrs. Ramsay's inner consciousness as she sits as hostess at dinner. She has been musing over her private problems when she becomes aware suddenly that one of her guests, William Bankes, had praised Scott's Waverley novels: "He read one of them every six months, he said. And why should that make Charles Tansley angry? He rushed in (all, thought Mrs. Ramsay, because Prue will not be nice to him) and denounced the Waverley novels when he knew nothing about it, nothing about it whatsoever. . . ."²² What the parentheses indicate here is a shift of levels of consciousness; it is not an extreme shift, to be sure, but in Virginia Woolf's typically subtle manner, a shift. Because her basic technique in this novel is indirect monologue, she finds it unnecessary to rely very often on such external devices as punctuation. When she does use them they are as clear and as natural as this example indicates.

Defying comparison with Virginia Woolf, in this and most other respects, is Waldo Frank. Frank's technical virtuosity is not very impressive; yet his experiments with stream-of-consciousness fiction are informative for a discussion of the possibilities within the genre. He relies more heavily on punctuation and typographical devices to control the movement of consciousness than does any other writer. Frank's dependence, for example in the novel *Rahab*, is on ellipses, dashes, and verse. So far as I can tell, he uses each of these for specific kinds of stream of consciousness: the ellipsis marks indicate visual or auditory images which fall on the character's inner consciousness; the dashes indicate abstracted reactions to these images; and the lines of verse (which are always used with a dash also) indicate an inchoate and highly emotional psychic reaction.

It is interesting that Joyce, whose use of devices is notorious, relies less on mechanical ones than any other stream-of-consciousness writer except Dorothy Richardson—who never had the technical challenges that Joyce did because she never attempted as much. The reason Joyce was able to waive this type of control is, of course, that he *did* have so many others at hand to accomplish the same ends. In two aspects, however, one positive and one negative, a consideration of *Ulysses* will further inform us of the function of typographical devices for controlling the movement of stream-of-consciousness fiction. The positive aspect is found in the "Aeolus" or "Cave of the Winds" episode (that one which takes place in the newspaper office). Here, Joyce's penchant for using montage is evident; for the entire episode consists of a series of brief events, physical and mental, which are connected only by their relation to the milieu of the press and editorial rooms of the newspaper. About half of the scenes are interior monologue passages. Joyce's device for knitting these passages together and for providing the reader with a key to them is a typographical one: it consists of newspaper headlines to introduce each one. The reader of twentieth-century fiction is familiar with this device in John Dos Passos' "Newsreel" sections in his trilogy, *USA*. There the purpose, broadly speaking, is to give diverse commentary on the follies of the world. Joyce's purposes are different from those of the American novelist. Only an example from the "Cave of the Winds" episode can show this purpose adequately. The headline for one "scene" reads: AND IT WAS THE FEAST OF THE PASSOVER; Leopold Bloom's monologue under that follows:

> He stayed in his walk to watch a typesetter neatly distributing type. Reads it backwards first. Quickly he does it. Must require some practice that. mangiD kcirtaP. Poor papa with his hagadah book, reading backwards with his finger to me. Pessach. Next year in Jerusalem. Dear, O dear! All that long business about that brought us out of the land of Egypt and into the house of bondage. *alleluia. Shema Israel Adonai Elohenu.* No that's the other. Then the twelve brothers, Jacob's sons. . . . [P. 121.]

This contemplation of Hebrew lore has no connection with the rest of the episode. It is merely another of the glimpses the reader gets into Bloom's consciousness, unified and made to seem logical by the device of the headline and the logic of the central association, the name Patrick Dignam, spelled right to left like Hebrew. The glimpse knits the entire episode by sustaining the confused and satirical tone and by giving a common starting point for the process of free association from scene to scene.

The negative aspect of Joyce's contribution to the use of typographical controls of stream-of-consciousness fiction is best illustrated in the previously quoted excerpts from Molly Bloom's monologue. It contains no punctuation. By omitting even the most basic punctuation and typographical aids, Joyce manages to present the flow which is typical of Molly's consciousness as it is represented on a near-sleep level. The lack of punctuation is entirely a visual control, for the monologue itself is actually carefully phrased.

Thus, even by purely external means, the flux of mental life can be represented and controlled in fiction. We have seen that the chief principle of the movement of consciousness is the common law of mental association. This has been recognized and exploited by the stream-of-consciousness writers. They have also borrowed devices from cinematic technique and have made special use of conventional punctuation in order to represent and control the stream. But flux is only one of the two obvious qualities of consciousness. The other is its privacy; that is, the unformulated and incoherent aspects which make any one consciousness an enigma to another. These two fundamental aspects of consciousness are closely connected and, we shall discover in the following chapter, they are both, in part, results of the mental laws of free association.

3

The Devices

One can never know directly the contents of the "unconscious."

S. FREUD

THE GREATEST PROBLEM of the stream-of-consciousness writer is to capture the irrational and incoherent quality of private unuttered consciousness and in doing so still to communicate to his readers. Readers in the twentieth century, after all, expect of language and syntax some kind of empirical order and completeness. Yet, if consciousness is to be represented at all convincingly, the representation must lack to a great degree these very qualities that a reader has a right to expect. The private consciousness has an entire file of symbols and associations which are confidential and are inscribed in secret code. Another consciousness ordinarily is not admitted to this file, and in addition, it has no key by which to decode what is there. The result is that to a great degree the materials of any one consciousness are an enigma to any other one. The purpose of literature is not to express enigmas. Consequently, the writer of stream-of-consciousness literature has to manage to represent consciousness realistically by maintaining its characteristics of privacy (the incoherence, discontinuity, and private implications), and he has to manage to communicate something to the reader through this consciousness. If he is a successful writer, he does this; and he must use ingenuity in doing it, although he has only the basic materials of language and syntax available to all writers and readers.

The Problem of Privacy

The most solid foundation of fictional technique is the convention of author omniscience. No matter what skill is displayed toward objectifying fiction, the omniscience of the author is naturally assumed. Such is art; but such is artifice that it attempts to conceal this basic convention. When we use such phrases as "author exit" and "dramatic immediacy," we are using hyperbole; but we are also commenting on the fact that there has been an attempt on the part of writers to convince their readers that what they present is actual existence—something the reader can accept as existing independent of the writer. Since no stream-of-consciousness writer has recorded, ostensibly, his own psychic processes, all stream-of-consciousness fiction is presented more or less objectively. That is, the author of a stream-of-consciousness novel is always presenting a created character's consciousness and not his own, no matter how autobiographical the bias is. Otherwise, he would not be responsible for created art, but he would be guilty of passing off "automatic writing" as fiction.

The writer of stream-of-consciousness fiction, like all serious writers, has something to say, some sense of values he wants to communicate to the reader. Unlike other writers, however, he chooses the internal world of psychic activity in which to dramatize these values. But psychic activity is a private thing and must be represented as private in order for the writer to gain reader-confidence. Consequently, the stream-of-consciousness writer has to do two things: (1) he has to represent the actual texture of consciousness, and (2) he has to distill some meaning from it for the reader. This presents a dilemma to the writer, because the nature of consciousness involves a private sense of values, private associations, and private relationships peculiar to that consciousness; therefore it is enigmatic to an outside consciousness.

Some writers have partly overcome the dilemma of sacrificing objectivity. Such are Dorothy Richardson and Virginia Woolf, whose techniques, we have seen, admit of author interference. These writers are therefore both less difficult to read and less effective as realists than James Joyce and William Faulkner, who are more objective. But all of the major stream-of-consciousness writers have employed the same basic devices to accomplish their purposes. The most important of these devices are: (1) suspension of mental content according to the laws of psychological association, (2) representation of discontinuity and compression by standard rhetorical figures, and (3) suggestion of multiple and extreme levels of meaning by images and symbols.

Since all of the writers under consideration use these devices in nearly the same way, we may concentrate for more clear illustration on excerpts from the novels of but one representative of the genre. I choose William Faulkner's work for illustration because he has a great deal to communicate, because he maintains an amazing objectivity, and because further explanation of his methods is still needed.

Excerpts from two of Faulkner's novels will serve for an analysis. The first is chosen because of its simplicity, since it is near the surface of consciousness; the other is deeper in consciousness and more complex. Let us examine first the beginning of one of Dewey Dell's soliloquies in the novel, *As I Lay Dying.*

> The signboard comes in sight. It is looking out at the road now, because it can wait. New Hope. 3 mi. it will say. New Hope. 3 mi. New Hope 3 mi. And then the road will begin, curving away into the trees, empty with waiting, saying New Hope three miles.
>
> I have heard that my mother is dead. I wish I had time to let her die. I wish I had time to wish I

had. It is because in the wild and outraged earth too soon too soon too soon. It's not that I wouldn't and will not it's that it is too soon too soon too soon.[1]

Out of context this seems truly enigmatic. But the reader knows a great deal about Dewey Dell's psyche on the eighty-ninth page of the novel, and he knows a few pertinent facts about her history: he knows that she is illegitimately pregnant; that she is a sensitive, if ignorant, seventeen-year-old girl; that she is a part of the outrageous spectacle of an obsessed family as it makes a pilgrimage to bury the not-too-recently deceased mother. In this soliloquy, she is distracted by her mother's death; but in addition, she is pregnant, and this is the chief cause of her anxiety. Yet, even with this knowledge of the situation and of Dewey Dell, most readers would find elements of incoherence, prolixity, and capriciousness in the passage; enough, at least, for them to be convinced that they were actually within the private realm of the consciousness of Dewey Dell.

When we consider a more complex passage from stream-of-consciousness fiction (more complex because the character is more complex and the level of consciousness is lower), we find the evidences of privacy more definite and the enigma more puzzling. This passage is a section of Quentin Compson's monologue in the second episode of *The Sound and the Fury*. He is approaching the hour of his planned suicide. He has just been down the corridor to the bathroom and he is returning to his room where he had shortly before cleaned a spot from his trousers with gasoline:

. . . I returned up the corridor, waking the lost feet in whispering battalions in the silence, into the gasoline, the watch telling its furious lie on the dark table. Then the curtains breathing out of the dark upon my face, leaving the breathing upon my face. A quarter hour yet. And then I'll not be. The peacefullest words. Peacefullest words. *Non fui. Sum. Fui. Non sum.* Somewhere I heard bells once.

Mississippi or Massachusetts. I was. I am not. Massachusetts or Mississippi. Shreve has a bottle in his trunk. *Aren't you even going to open it* Mr and Mrs Jason Richmond Compson announce the *Three Times. Days. Aren't you even going to open it* marriage of their daughter Candace *that liquor teaches you to confuse the means with the end.* I am. Drink. I was not. Let us sell Benjy's pasture so that Quentin may go to Harvard and I may knock my bones together and together. I will be dead in. Was it one year Caddy said.[2]

From these two examples, let us discover what we can of how stream-of-consciousness writers go about representing the effect of the privacy of consciousness and how they manage to make it all meaningful to the reader.

Suspended Coherence

What seems incoherent in the privacy of consciousness is actually only egocentric. The basis for this is the private relationships of the associations. Thus we have again to consider the functioning of free association in stream-of-consciousness fiction. We have seen in a previous chapter that free association is the chief principle by which the movement of any "'stream" of consciousness is controlled. It is a stabilizing factor, although a tenuous one. Often in *Ulysses,* for example, the associations are not explained at the time the process is indicated. The explanations may lie hidden several hundred pages separated from the association. Consequently, at the moment the association is made, unless the reader has a remarkable memory, the effect is one of incoherence. There will seem to be simply no logical reason for such a connection. The reason lies in the seeming lack of logic of psychological free association and in the egocentricity with which it functions in the psychic processes.

When Molly Bloom, for example, in her monologue, associates her imagined argument with an atheist with her courtship by Leopold (see p. 46, above), there is an element of seeming incoherence. There is no obvious or even evocative connection between the two for the reader; but there is for Molly. Of course, Joyce, in this instance, is careful to give enough of the specific image in Molly's mind to make what is actually illogical come clear for the reader. Likewise, when Virginia Woolf has Clarissa Dalloway concerned with her hat while she is sympathizing with Hugh Whitbread because of his wife's "slight indisposition" (see p. 51, above), the connection doesn't make sense (except for Clarissa) until Virginia Woolf explains the whole process a few lines later.

This method of suspending sense impressions and ideas in the memory for so long that they reappear at unexpected and seemingly unreasonable places is also used by Faulkner to preserve the appearance of privacy. Actually, it works so as to give the alert reader something to hold on to. In the Dewey Dell passage above, the basis for the enigma is the privacy of the central association. Why, for example, does Dewey Dell think of a signboard as waiting? It is not in the ordinary person's mind to make this association; but it is in Dewey Dell's, not because she is more of a poet than the ordinary person and has trained herself to think in symbols, but because she, privately, is confronted with a pressing problem. It is so pressing that she dare not, though she must, wait to solve it. The static repose of the signboard reminds her of this problem. It is the one inanimate object which at the moment comes to her attention. It fuses with the thing predominant in her consciousness, her illegitimate pregnancy, which she believes she must check immediately. She can not wait. Although the privacy quality of the passage is achieved, the meaning can be grasped easily after one has "caught on" to the method.

In the passage above from Quentin Compson's monologue, the functioning of association to produce the incoherency of consciousness is more complex and thorough. In this short passage, many phrases which may seem incoherent can be understood by analysis from the principle that they are egocentric associations and the key to them is elsewhere in the novel—since Faulkner is a responsible writer. For example, "Waking the lost feet," because it is a familiar figure of speech (synecdoche), is fairly clear in itself; but it is more meaningful if the reader has in mind the impression [given on page 190, Modern Library Edition] Quentin has when he treads the same hall earlier: ". . . just the stairs curving up into shadows echoes of feet in the sad generations like light dust upon the shadows, my feet waking them like dust, lightly to settle again." "The watch telling its furious lie," an expressive figure of speech in itself (personification) demands, for full impact, recall of Quentin's father's lectures to him when the parent presented the son with a watch: "Quentin, I give you the mausoleum of all hope and desire; it's rather excrutiating-ly apt that you will use it to gain the reducto absurdum of all human experience. . . ."

A more notable example is the way "a quarter hour yet" fits significantly into the pattern of Quentin's thought. The alert reader knows this because he has had such clues as "and wrote the two notes and sealed them" on page 100, and the fact given on page 104 of Quentin's buying two six-pound flatirons—the alert reader is finally aware that the protagonist actually intends to leave for the river to commit suicide in fifteen minutes. The fact that it is to be at a certain moment ("a quarter hour yet") is one of the obsessions Quentin has to twist his crucial act further from the normal.

The seemingly irrelevant "somewhere I heard bells once" is explained by the fact that the ringing of bells has impinged on Quentin's consciousness at various intervals throughout the account of his preparations for suicide. We are prepared to recognize that there is a symbolic meaning to "bells" on two levels for Quentin: they are wedding bells for his sister Candace, and they are college chimes ringing out the quarter-hours as the time approaches for the suicide. On page 98 there is this key to the bell motif: "It was a while before the last stroke ceased vibrating. It stayed in the air, more felt than heard, for a long time. Like all the bells that ever rang still ringing in the long dying light-rays and Jesus and Saint Francis talking about his sister."

"That liquor teaches you to confuse the means with the ends" bears a private meaning for Quentin: his father, who is inextricably involved in the incestual illusion Quentin has for his sister, is referred to in the immediately preceding thought—he is "Mr Jason Richmond Compson." The reader, who has been prepared for the father's penchant for sententious sayings by such things as: "It's always the idle habits you acquire which you will regret" and "it used to be a gentleman was known by his books; nowadays he is known by the ones he has not returned"—the reader realizes that the phrase "liquor teaches you to confuse the means with the ends" is an epigram echoing from the father, and it crazily impinges on Quentin's consciousness at this point.

What Faulkner has done in this passage is what he has done all the way through *The Sound and the Fury* (and it is what most stream-of-consciousness writers have done) to present the inherent discontinuity of psychic processes and to make it meaningful. We may think of it this way: As the associations of any particular moment of consciousness are incoherent out of the context of the mind, so the associations in the passage above are incoherent out of the context of the novel; but within the context of the novel, they are not only psychologically coherent, they are revealing. The novelists have used the basic principles of psychological free association as their guide. The associations which Quentin follows are nonsense out of context of the novel and are at first puzzling to the casual reader. The point is thus made by the author that at least the reader is actually within the character's mind here. But since Faulkner and Joyce and Woolf and some others do not write nonsensical fiction, they have carefully dropped clues to unravel the knots of privacy throughout their work. In short, for the responsible writer, the mind of the character is the mind which exists *in the novel*.

The use of free association as a method for conveying the privacy aspect of the psychic processes is not always so abstruse as this. It is much simpler, but just as private, for example, when Benjy, the idiot brother of Quentin and Candace, in the opening pages of *The Sound and the Fury* hears the golfer call "caddie!" and immediately thinks of his sister Candace whose nickname is Caddy; then his idiot's mind reverts to an incident eighteen years earlier when his adored Caddy was with him.

In *Ulysses* also, free association is sometimes operating on a fairly simple level, although it always conveys the effect of privacy. Following is a fairly typical example. Leopold Bloom is strolling along in Dublin and sees a billboard announcing a performance of *Leah* with the actress Mrs. Bandman Palmer. His psyche rambles on as follows:

> Like to see her in that again. Hamlet she played last night. Male impersonator. Perhaps he was a woman. Why Ophelia committed suicide? Poor Papa! How he used to talk about Kate Bateman in that! Outside the Adelphi in London waited all afternoon to get in. Year before I was born that was: sixty-five. [P. 75.]

Here the purely private association of "papa" with Ophelia is, as most readers would guess, the fact that Leopold Bloom's father also committed suicide. The memory of this is off and on in Leopold's mind throughout the day. It becomes intricately connected with various themes throughout the book, but this is the first hint of it.

The use of free association by Virginia Woolf, both as a control of the movement and direction of her characters' "streams" and as a method for indicating the privacy factor of consciousness, is conditioned by her special method of indirect interior monologue. It has been noted in another chapter that the characteristic feature of this technique is the definite author guidance of the stream. Because of this author interference, Virginia Woolf relies on the principle of association even more boldly than do most stream-of-consciousness writers. It is important to her to convince the reader of the privacy of the material, since actually she makes everything so clear. As David Daiches has pointed out, she has a special signal for any turn in the direction of the psychic flow and for any point at which a private association enters.[3] This signal is a combination of the use of the word "for" as an illative conjunction with the use of the ambiguous pronoun "one." The opening pages of *Mrs. Dalloway* again serve best for illustration because the reader does not have to depend on previous exposition, yet he is plunged directly into Clarissa's thought stream. Ellipsis marks will be used generously in the following quotation in order to give a full example of this special method in a small space. The italics are mine.

Mrs. Dalloway said she would buy the flowers herself.

For Lucy had her work cut out for her . . . and then, thought Clarissa Dalloway, what a morning —fresh as if issued to children on a beach.

What a lark! What a plunge! *For* so it had always seemed to her, when, with a little squeak of the hinges . . . she had plunged at Bourton into the open air . . . Peter Walsh! He would be back from India one of these days, June or July, she forgot which *for* his letters were awfully dull; it was his sayings *one* remembered. . . .

She stiffened a little on the kerb . . . waiting to cross, very upright.

For having lived in Westminster . . . *one* feels even in the midst of traffic . . . an indescribable pause . . . before Big Ben strikes. . . . Such fools we are. . . . *For* Heaven only knows why

> *one* loves it so, how *one* sees it so . . . life; London; this moment of June.
>
> *For* it was the middle of June. . . .

This is of course uninteresting, telescoped as it is, but the use of "for" to indicate both turns in direction and the individualized associations becomes clear. Even the "for" in "for his letters were awfully dull" is used in this manner, although it is also used here in its ordinary causal function. The use of "one" emphasizes the privacy, yet allows the author to keep the reader under a guiding leash.

Discontinuity

In addition to the basic method of free association, writers employ other devices to achieve the tone and texture of private consciousness. These can be classified under the general term "rhetorical devices." Let us look back to the Dewey Dell soliloquy from *As I Lay Dying* for an example of this. The passage begins with figurative language: the signboard is said to be looking and waiting. The personification is continued and hyperbaton (violation of the usual order of words) is added in "New Hope. 3 mi. it will say." The device of repetition is then used and there follows in quick order the use of metaphor, personification again, more repetition, litotes, irony, anacoluthon (a change of construction leaving the first part of the sentence broken: "It is because in the wild and outraged earth too soon too soon too soon"), anaphora (repetition of a word or form at the beginning of clauses: It's not . . . It's that it is . . ."), and perhaps others which do not need to be pointed out except to emphasize the point.

We should keep in mind that practically any passage of writing, in any genre, contains rhetorical figures in abundance, for they are natural and commonplace. Here, it is the piling up of them, the over-all use of *incrementum* that is unique and that, because it indicates a need for close reading and gives an enigmatic tone to the passage, serves to heighten the effect of the privacy of the materials.

If we wish to see the method carried further, we need only turn to the passage above from Quentin's monologue in *The Sound and the Fury*. In this passage, it is the extensive use of discontinuity that sets the tone. A number of rhetorical figures have already been pointed out in this passage (above, in relation to the use of private associations), but the chief rhetorical devices are those which indicate discontinuity: epanodos, ellipsis, anaphora, anacoluthon, dislocated parenthesis, and brachylogy. Most of these are not common to ordinary prose, yet the quality they indicate—discontinuity—is inherent enough in psychic functioning to provide a further mark of verisimilitude to the already established incoherency factor of the passage. In addition, these devices give a further logical basis for interpreting the passage. This basis depends on the recognition that rhetorical figures are merely formal labels for common thought patterns inherent in the various special demands of word communication. Thus the figures have an empirical logic. As a result, when we read "Mississippi or Massachusetts . . . Massachusetts or Mississippi" it is not an entirely ludicrous or unreasonable thing, despite its overtones of incoherence, because the figure is a familiar one (although the classical name for it may not be: it is epanodos combined with alliteration). So it is also when the reader comes across "Aren't you even going to open it Mr and Mrs Jason Richmond Compson announce the . . . Aren't you even going to open it marriage of their daughter" (anaphora), or when he encounters "Mr and Mrs Jason Richmond Compson announce the three times" (anacoluthon).

This extreme use of figurative language and of classical rhetorical devices is a characteristic of stream-of-consciousness fiction. When it is used as consciously as Faulkner here uses it, it is not used as rhetorical decoration and embroidery. There is a function for it and that function is to heighten the sense of discontinuity in the privacy of psychic processes.

At this point, it is necessary to consider the use of these devices in *Ulysses*, chiefly because Joyce is almost notorious for his command of them—this notoriety is owing primarily to the research done by Stuart Gilbert on the "Aeolus" episode. Gilbert says,

> The thirty-two pages of this episode comprise a veritable thesaurus of rhetorical devices and might, indeed, be adopted as a text-book for students of the art of rhetoric. Professor Bain has remarked that in the course of the plays, 'Shakespeare exemplifies nearly every rhetorical artifice known.' Doubtless this might be said of any copious writer . . . whose work extends over decades and scores of volumes, but the gathering together under the pen within the space of thirty-two pages, in the one episode of *Ulysses* which deals exclusively with rhetoric, of nearly all the important, misleading enthymemes elenchated by Quintilian and his successors, and the making out of such elenchation a lively organic part of a very living organism, is a hoax of quite another colour.[4]

He then lists ninety-five examples of different devices in this episode. This is impressive, and commentators on Joyce have signaled Gilbert's statement out time after time. But Joyce's display of rhetoric here is greatly a tour de force, and it is not intrinsically bound to the stream-of-consciousness functioning of the novel. What is not so well publicized and is more remarkable is Joyce's less self-conscious use of rhetorical devices in sections of his novel which are concerned with his primary purpose of depicting inner states. In these places, rhetoric is used not for its own sake, but as a device for capturing the actuality of psychic processes; it is a device for producing the texture of discontinuity that is a quality of consciousness. As an example, the following bit of interior monologue of Stephen's, which opens the "Proteus" epi-

74

sode of *Ulysses*, contains, as does the example above from Faulkner, the special devices of discontinuity.

Ineluctable modality of the visible [epigram]: at least that if no more, thought through my eyes [metaphor]. Signatures of all things I am here to read [hyperbaton], seaspawn and seawrack, the nearing tide, that rusty boot. Snotgreen, bluesilver, rust: coloured signs. Limits of the diaphane. But he adds: in bodies. Then he was aware of them bodies before of them coloured [anastrophe]. How? By knocking his sconce against them, sure [dialect]. Go easy, Bald he was and a millionaire *maestro di color che sanno*. Limit of the diaphane in. Why in? Diaphane, adiaphane [euphony]. If you can put your five fingers through it, it is a gate [enthymeme], if not a door. Shut your eyes and see.

Stephen closed his eyes to hear his boots [synesthesia] crush crackling wrack and shells [onomatopoeia]. You are walking through it howsomever. I am, a stride at a time. A very short space of time through very short times of space [chiasmus]. Five, six, the *nacheinander*. Exactly: and that is the ineluctable modality of the audible. Open your eyes. No. Jesus! If I fell over a cliff that beetles o'er his base, fell through the *nebeneinander* ineluctably [protasis] I am getting on nicely in the dark. My ash sword hangs at my side. Tap with it: they do. My two feet in his boots are at the end of his legs [metonomy], *nebeneinander*. Sounds solid: made by the mallet of *Los Demiurgos*. Am I walking into eternity along Sandymount strand? Crush, crick, crick, crick [alliteration and onomatopoeia]. Wild sea money. Dominie Deasy kens [archaism] them a'.

> Won't you come to Sandymount,
> Madeline the mare?

Rhythm begins, you see. I hear [brachylogy]. A catelectic tetrameter of iams marching [personification]. No, agallop [archaism]: *deline the mare* [ellipsis].

I have in this short passage indicated twenty instances of the use of rhetorical figures and devices. There are probably as many more that could be found. I suspect that Joyce seldom did so well in the "Aeolus" episode, which was consciously devoted to them.

This use of rhetorical figures is a feature, then, of stream-of-consciousness writing which stems naturally from the attempt to reproduce the broken, seemingly incoherent, disjointed texture of the processes of consciousness when they are not deliberately screened for direct communication. To a degree, but in a less concentrated fashion, the same thing can be found in Virginia Woolf's and Dorothy Richardson's novels. But the kind of connotative meaning these two writers depend upon most is achieved by the more familiar devices of images and symbols.

Transformation by Metaphor

An image is, of course, a rhetorical device, used in all effective writing, by which a sense impression is conveyed. Images can be identified as figurative comparisons, usually in the form of similes or metaphors. The poetic and richly wrought texture which imagery produces is found in such diverse works as the undifferentiated meanderings of *Pilgrimage*, the highly ordered and contrived *Ulysses*, the subtle and rarefied "transparent envelope" which is *Mrs. Dalloway*, and the dense rhetoric of *The Sound and the Fury*—as well as in the either banal or chaotic products of the less successful stream-of-consciousness writers. A general accounting for the great use of imagery in stream-of-consciousness fiction has to be on the same basis which explains the great use of rhetorical devices in general: the attempt by writers to overcome the dilemma which confronts them in trying to present private consciousness.

We do not need laboratory tests to convince us that

there are feelings and impressions which the human mind cannot successfully verbalize. To what degree this is so depends on the particular mind in any particular situation. Poets, because they usually are trying to communicate something so precise or so subjective that it evades denotative language, have always relied upon comparisons to express what they mean. The stream-of-consciousness writer is exploring the very area in which the rationalizing process of verbalization is not involved. His dilemma is that he has chosen words to express this nonverbal area of the mind. Like the poet, he has resorted to the convention of using comparisons.

But the dilemma is not completely solved that easily. The stream-of-consciousness writer's problem is different from the poet's because the former has the task of retaining the appearances of the confusion of the nonverbal psychic processes. This confusion is marked by being fragmentary more than by anything else; that is, it lacks the rational aspect of normal syntax which is fundamentally achieved by a conventional subject-object relationship. In order to give the appearance of this lack of normal syntactical completeness and at the same time to express what is beyond the power of denotative meaning, stream-of-consciousness writers have employed images in two particular ways: they have used the image impressionistically, and they have used symbolism.

By impressionist use of imagery, I mean the description of an immediate perception in figurative terms which expand to express an emotional attitude toward a more complex thing. A good example is Dewey Dell's impression of the signboard as "looking out at the road now, because it can wait." The methods of expansion vary and they will be illustrated presently. We shall find that the writers who characteristically use imagery in this manner are those who are frequently labeled impressionists—those, in short, who are most subjective in their method, and they are Dorothy Richardson and

Virginia Woolf. By "symbolism," I mean simply the considerable use of symbols. A symbol is a truncated metaphor; that is, it is a metaphor with the first term lacking. Consequently, it is a device for concentrating the expression of a comparison; it is at the same time, of course, like all metaphor, a device for expanding meaning. Both image and symbol tend to express something of the quality of privacy in consciousness: the image by suggesting the private emotional values of what is perceived (either directly, through memory, or through imagination); the symbol by suggesting the truncated manner of perceiving and the expanded meaning. It can be seen that the symbolist's method as it is used in stream-of-consciousness fiction is closely allied with the naturalist's attempt to present his material exactly. The two writers, Joyce and Faulkner, who depend most on symbolism, are most frequently placed in the naturalistic tradition of the novel.

The stream-of-consciousness fiction which relies most on imagery is Dorothy Richardson's *Pilgrimage*. We have seen that her basic technique is the unusual one of merely describing psychic being. It is by relying on imagery that she gives this any of the necessary effect of privacy. The author (and one has the idea that she closely identifies herself with the protagonist, Miriam Henderson) for the most part simply describes the impressions which Miriam encounters and states the associations which Miriam has with these initial impressions. This is done usually in terms of imagery, not narrative. It is concrete, not abstract; and it is reflective, not dramatic. Dorothy Richardson handles this approach so skillfully that the reader comes to identify images with certain moods of the character, and he comes to be able to fill in the blank spaces in Miriam's own private psyche.

A passage from *Honeycomb*, the third volume of *Pilgrimage*, will illustrate the functioning of imagery in stream-of-consciousness fiction. Miriam is having lunch in the house where she is governess. There are several men, guests of her employer, eating lunch also at a nearby table. Miriam's impression of them follows:

> Miriam's stricken eyes sought their foreheads for relief. Smooth brows and neatly brushed hair above; but the smooth motionless brows were ramparts of hate; pure murderous hate. That's men, she said, with a sudden flash of certainty, that's men as they are, when they are opposed, when they are real. All the rest is pretence. Her thoughts flashed forward to a final clear issue of opposition, with a husband. Just a cold blank hating forehead and neatly brushed hair above it. If a man doesn't understand or doesn't agree he's just a blank bony conceitedly thinking, absolutely condemning forehead, a face below, going on eating—and going off somewhere. Men are all hard angry bones; always thinking something, only one thing at a time and unless that is agreed to, they murder. My husband shan't kill me. . . . I'll shatter his conceited brow —*make* him see . . . two sides to every question . . . a million sides . . . no questions, only sides . . . always changing. Men argue, think they prove things; their foreheads recover—cool and calm. Damn them all—all men.[5]

This is omniscient description of what Miriam is thinking, except for the last few lines, which break into direct interior monologue. The "she said," for example, doesn't mean "she said," but it means more than "she thought," because the author is attempting a direct transcript of the texture of Miriam's thoughts. This is done by imagery, by presenting the impressions that flash through Miriam's mind in terms of images that are typical, almost inevitable, to the kind of person she is. "Just a cold blank hating forehead and neatly brushed hair above it"—this is man, the male, for Miriam. Her image of him as he is eating is her image of him as always a potential "issue of opposition"; it is her image of him as "my husband." John

Cowper Powys in his book on Dorothy Richardson might have used this example as evidence for what he considers her great achievement as a writer: the presentation of life from a feminine point of view.[6] Or Professor Beach might have indicated it to underscore his idea that Miriam's psychological obsession is with men. Although Beach says she never "draws it up to light," yet she comes exceedingly close to it here.[7]

What we can deduce from Dorothy Richardson's method is that she presents Miriam's impressions of things as Miriam has these impressions, and the images in which they are presented imply much about what is going on in Miriam's consciousness. Her obsession with men is implied in the above excerpt. We have Miriam's impressions of things in terms of imagery, and as readers, we have impressions of Miriam from our imaginative interpretation of these images.

A different use of imagery is found commonly in stream-of-consciousness writing. For example, there is in *Ulysses* a heavy use of imagery. It functions there more narrowly, and it usually is in terms of symbols. When, for illustration, Stephen remembers his traumatic experience at his mother's deathbed, it is presented to the reader in the following image-ridden passage:

> In a dream, silently, she had come to him, her wasted body within its loose graveclothes giving off an odour of wax and rosewood, her breath bent over him with mute secret words, a faint odour of wetted ashes.
>
> Her glazing eyes, staring out of death, to shake and bend my soul. On me alone. The ghostcandle to light her agony. Ghostly light on the tortured face. Her hoarse loud breath rattling in horror, while all prayed on their knees. Her eyes on me to strike me down. [P. 12.]

Here, it is not impressionism which results, but it is the imagist's desire to present particulars exactly. Because the particulars are psychological phenomena, these private images (combined with the intense rhetoric) come as close as imaginable to an exact rendering of the phenomena—unless it were to be in terms from the psychoanalyst's chamber.[8]

The basis of symbolism is the use of special and private symbols. Edmund Wilson in his important study of Symbolism says that "the symbols of the Symbolist School are usually chosen arbitrarily by the poet to stand for special ideas of his own—they are a sort of disguise for these ideas."[9] We might paraphrase and say that the symbols of the stream-of-consciousness writers are usually chosen deliberately by the writers to convince the reader of the privacy and the actuality of the mind being represented, as well as to stand for ideas peculiar to that mind.

Modern artists, and particularly those writers who have been concerned with mental functioning, have recognized, either from theory, or what is more likely, from self-conscious experience, that the primary mental process is that of forming symbols. From simple perceptions and feelings come symbols; and this symbol-forming process is prior to association or ideation. This theory has been explored analytically and logically by a number of contemporary philosophers (Cassirer, Whitehead, and Langer, for example), but it has been documented directly by the stream-of-consciousness writers. It is important to an understanding of the system of "writing down" mental content to be aware of this responsible reason for the use of symbolization.

Symbols and symbolism loom large in any concept of modern literary methods. Much has been written about the subject and much more assumed; and most of this has been distressingly generalized. I would add this to the assumptions and the generalizations: The chief impetus for reliance on symbols is rooted in the psychological experience which indicates that symbolization is a primary mental process. The worst result of general awareness of this has been that much twentieth-century symbolic art has lost its footing, and there have developed various irresponsible surrealistic trends in which symbols are the end and not the means. On the contrary, stream-of-consciousness literature has used symbols realistically and methodically. At least it has used them this way in its attempt to present mental functioning as primarily symbol-making. Thus, in attempting to discover how writers present the mind as convincingly unsimplified, as realistic, we find the use of symbol-making a key to the method.[10]

A great deal of the effect Joyce gets in such writing comes from the symbolic force of the images. In the passage from Stephen's consciousness quoted above, the image of his mother appears as a symbol. It stands for Stephen's remorse for his refusal to obey his mother's dying wish. The term Stephen himself gives to this feeling is "Agenbite of Inwit." Remorse is one of the chief themes of the book. It is not confined to Stephen's stricken conscience in relation only to his mother. That is only one aspect of it, for Stephen is conscience-stricken about a number of things, among which are his neglect of his sisters, his inability to settle on any values, and chiefly, his alienation from the Church in which he was reared. The dying-mother scene, which recurs eight times in the novel according to Kain's compilation, is a symbol for all of this.[11]

There are literally hundreds of other images used as symbols in *Ulysses*. A few examples, merely from the one episode from which the above passage is taken (the opening episode), will show how they are used and how frequently they occur. The scene opens with Buck Mulligan coming forth "bearing a bowl of lather on which a mirror and razor lay crossed"; he intones *Introibo ad altare Dei*. The image of course is a symbol of blasphemous ritual, specifically that of sacrifice. Later, Stephen looks out over the bay and the image in his mind is: "The ring of bay and skyline held a dull green mass of liquid."

This becomes also a symbol (through the processes of association) for the bowl which stood by his mother's bed, "holding the green sluggish bile." These two image-symbols are concentrations of the expression of Stephen's far-reaching remorse. With the kind of sensitivity and conscience which Stephen has, all images which impinge on his mind are symbols for his great remorse; a remorse he avoids by cynicism in his words, but cannot avoid in his consciousness; indeed, a remorse Joyce cannot express in words, but which he can express in the symbolic force of images.

Thus one aspect of the use of symbols in the literature under discussion can be seen to derive from the naturalists' attempt to present objective reality. For example, in the Dewey Dell soliloquy quoted above—as well as in the Quentin monologue—it can be seen immediately that the symbol is forming in the character's mind before any association or any beginning of ideation comes. Dewey Dell perceives the signboard and it impinges on her mind with symbolic shape. Naturally, the symbol is not defined, since symbols are by nature indefinable; but the reader is enough conscious *with* the character to find the symbol-making process fully believable and partly meaningful. The associations and the ideas come later in Dewey Dell's mind—and in the reader's—after the symbol is formed. Much the same is true in the Quentin monologue, although the symbol-making process is more active and even more private. The symbols there, the corridor, the lost-feet, the watch, the bells, and so forth, come before the associations, because they are the very things associated.

Other stream-of-consciousness writers use both the expressionistic image and the symbolic image in manners similar to Dorothy Richardson and Joyce. Further examples are not necessary to indicate the value of this poetic device for expressing what in consciousness cannot be expressed by direct communication, but must be expressed impressionistically or symbolically.

As we have seen, stream-of-consciousness writers have, in one way or another, devised workable methods for representing and controlling the subject matter which concerns them. The flow, the special time sense, and the enigma of consciousness are at once captured and communicated in a fictional context. But literary art, as Aristotle has told us, demands more than verisimilitude and clarity—it demands harmony. With motive and external action replaced by psychic being and functioning, what is to unify the fiction? What is to replace conventional plot?

4

The Forms

> *All I will do is to state a possibility. If human nature does alter it will be because individuals manage to look at themselves in a new way. Here and there people—a very few people, but a few novelists are among them—are trying to do this.*
>
> E. M. FORSTER

THE PROBLEM OF form for the stream-of-consciousness novelist is the problem of how order is imposed on disorder. He sets out to depict what is chaotic (human consciousness at an inchoate level) and is obligated to keep his depiction from being chaotic (to make a work of art). We may look at the problem in the following manner: if an author wishes to create a character by presenting that character's mind to the reader, then the work in which this is done has per se as its setting the character's mind. It has as its time of taking place the range of the characters' memories and fancies in time; it has as its place of action wherever the characters' minds wish to go in fancy or memory; and it has as its action whatever remembered, perceived, or imagined event the characters happen to focus on. In brief, the writer commits himself to dealing faithfully with what he conceives to be the chaos and accident of a consciousness—unpatterned, undisciplined, and unclear.

Art, the art of fiction, demands pattern, discipline, and clarity. The reader of fiction demands these things, and he must have them in order to have his own undisciplined consciousness focused and in order to be able to understand and interpret. Consequently, the writer must somehow impose pattern, or form, on his material. The chief of the conventional ways of doing this in fiction is by utilizing a unity of action and character; that is, by plot. But the stream-of-consciousness writer is not usually concerned with plot of action in the ordinary sense; he is concerned with psychic processes and not physical actions. If, then, the stream-of-consciousness writer cannot draw on the conventional use of plot to provide a necessary unity, he must devise other methods. He has done so and he has been exceedingly ingenious in doing it. This accounts for the unusual reliance on formal patterns which is found in the works of writers of stream-of-consciousness fiction.[1] These patterns can be classified according to several types:

1. The unities (time, place, character, and action)
2. Leitmotifs
3. Previously established literary patterns (burlesques)
4. Symbolic structures
5. Formal scenic arrangements
6. Natural cyclical schemes (seasons, tides, etc.)
7. Theoretical cyclical schemes (musical structures, cycles of history, etc.)

This is an arbitrary classification, made only to add convenience to an examination of the patterns. For example, the unities could easily be construed under either the heading "theoretical cyclical schemes" or even under "natural cyclical schemes."

We have explained the basis for a need for patterns in stream-of-consciousness fiction, but there still remains the problem of determining on what principles the patterns are used. In other words, we may ask this question: What specifically do patterns accomplish in stream-of-consciousness fiction? The question needs to be asked and answered because a very great deal is said by commentators about this unusual aspect of such novels as *Ulysses* and *Mrs. Dalloway,* but little is offered as an explanation for it. The method for examining these patterns will be to consider the works of the chief stream-of-consciousness writers, beginning with Joyce's *Ulysses,* in which all the classes of patterns are used, and ending with Dorothy Richardson's *Pilgrimage,* in which only one class is used.

Joyce's Daedal Network

That amazing book, *Ulysses,* is not the least amazing for being the most designed novel ever written. Not only does Joyce find employment in it for all seven of the categories of patterns, but within some of the categories he utilizes schemes never found in literature before his novel. These we shall consider presently. First, we ought to determine what there is about the book that justifies such extreme emphasis on design. It is not enough to say that it is almost plotless. It is necessary to add that it is dealing with what is, as a thing in itself, chaotic and difficult to interpret—it is dealing with human consciousness—and to add further that Joyce does attempt to interpret and to say something about life, and he expects the reader to understand and to interpret what he is saying.

The content of a psyche has no meaning in itself for another consciousness; it is too unformed, undisciplined; it offers no essential point of reference; it has no specific ordering; it is capricious and fluid; it offers, in short, no basis for analysis and interpretation. Consequently, and this is crucial to an understanding of stream-of-consciousness fiction, any novel which has as its purpose the depiction of psyche must remain faithful to the elasticity, the range, and the whimsy of that psyche. Any such novel is subject to formlessness and, in a sense, meaninglessness. This is true of *Ulysses*, and it is true of all other stream-of-consciousness novels.

In *Ulysses*, Stephen Dedalus' highly disciplined powers of reasoned communication come from a consciousness even more chaotic, because it is more complex, than is Leopold Bloom's. With both characters, Joyce is bound to adhere to the actual characteristics of their psyches as he has created them. His subject matter, then, contains no form. But his novel must contain it if a reader is to understand or if he, the creator of a literary work, is to communicate. The novelist must provide a frame of reference for interpretation, a device for differentiation and variation, and a means for getting lights and shadows; in short, the novelist must superimpose form on his formless subject matter. Joyce succeeds so well and uses so many patterns to give order to his material that too often the patterns overshadow the basic materials. Interesting in this respect is how much has been written to explain the particular patterns in *Ulysses*,[2] and how little has been said about the whole stream-of-consciousness function of the novel.

Some of the most important and in some ways the most interesting means Joyce uses to compensate for lack of plot and for the intricacies of presenting character on the level of psychic processes are the unities of time and place. *Ulysses* takes place on one day (eighteen hours) and in one city. Again, commentators have examined and pursued this aspect of the book so well that it is unnecessary to do it here, except to indicate the main features.

The narrative of *Ulysses* opens in two places: first, with the beginning of the day (June 16, 1904) for Stephen in the Martello Tower in the first episode of the novel; and next, with the beginning of the day in the Bloom household in the fourth episode. The time of day for both of these events is about the same (eight to ten o'clock). The progression of the episodes then follows in almost an hour-by-hour sequence: the second episode concerns Stephen's class at about ten o'clock; the third episode has Stephen contemplating on Sandymount Strand at about eleven o'clock; the fifth episode concerns Leopold at the Public Baths at ten; the sixth is the scene of the funeral at eleven; in the seventh episode, both Stephen and Leopold appear at a newspaper office at noon; in the eighth episode, Leopold has lunch at 1:00 P.M.; in the ninth episode, both Leopold and Stephen show up at the Dublin National Library at two; in the tenth episode there are glimpses of Leopold and Stephen in the Dublin bookstalls at three; the eleventh, twelfth, and thirteenth episodes concern Leopold's activities between four and eight; the fourteenth episode brings Leopold and Stephen together at the hospital in the evening; the fifteenth carries them together to the brothel at about midnight; the sixteenth has them at a cab shelter sobering up in the early morning; and the seventeenth sees them together at Bloom's house at about 2:00 A.M.; the last episode concerns Molly Bloom just after two.[3]

This all takes place in the city of Dublin and all from the point of view of but three characters. The detail with which Dublin is represented and the importance of it in relation to an interpretation of the whole novel is explored thoroughly by Richard Kain in his book on *Ulysses*. The significance of this amazing adherence to the triad of unities has not been investigated so far as the stream-of-consciousness function of the novel is concerned.

In order to investigate it, the first thing that must be understood is that, in one sense, the unities are not adhered to at all in *Ulysses*. Consider, for example, the number of minor characters; the many and far-removed geographical settings: Paris, Gibraltar, India, England; and especially consider the broad expanse of time that is covered by the action in the novel: Stephen's college days, his time in Paris; Leopold's childhood, his early married life; Molly's life as a girl, her courtship, her many affairs of the past few years. Yet, we say *Ulysses* is designed to adhere strictly to the unities because it takes place in one city, in less than one day, and involves three characters. There is of course no contradiction here. Adherence to the unities and the lack of it exist together in *Ulysses*. It all depends on how one considers the narrative: does it take place in the minds of the characters, or is it the thin surface action, the external odyssey of Bloom? The former lacks the unities; the latter adheres to them.

Since *Ulysses* is a stream-of-consciousness novel, since it has as its subject the psychic life of the characters, the chief action and the fundamental narrative do take place in the minds of the characters. There, unity is impossible simply because of the nature of the psyche: it is not neatly organized, and it is free of conventional time and space concepts. Consequently, this work of art which attempts to be faithful to the nature of psychic processes has to have form thrust upon it. This is the reason that Joyce's extreme adherence to the unities in his superficial narrative serves such an important function for his novel. It becomes a point of reference for following and interpreting the chaotic psyches he depicts. Further, it emphasizes the nature of these psyches by establishing a contrast of rigid form to their formlessness.

There are still other devices for gaining formal order in *Ulysses*. One that is predominant is the use of motif. The motif in *Ulysses* is important because it is pervading and it carries many minor themes; as a result, it adds the weight of meaning to the processes of consciousness depicted in the book. "Leitmotif" is a term borrowed from music, specifically from Wagnerian musical drama. It means, according to one standard American dictionary, "a marked melodic phrase or short passage, expressive of, or associated with, a certain idea, person, or situation, and accompanying its reappearance." Transferred to literary terms it may be defined as a recurring image, symbol, word, or phrase which carries a static association with a certain idea or theme. Beyond the relation explicit in these definitions, musical motifs and Joyce's literary motifs have little in common, and an analogy should not be carried further.

Joyce's motifs may be classed as image, symbol, or word-phrase motifs. They serve to carry minor themes throughout the novel and to express, with the power of image and symbol, what is in the minds of the characters. Most of all, they serve as formal links to aid in holding together the scattered materials of consciousness.

An example of the image-motif in *Ulysses* is the image Stephen frequently has of his dying mother. It is an obsession with him because he had refused her request to pray for her, and it is associated with his awareness of his spiritual exile. This is Stephen's "Agenbite of Inwit," his remorse of conscience; it serves as an emphasis of his attitude (*"non servium"*) warring with his spiritual kinship to mankind in general and love of his mother in particular. The motif first enters in the opening episode: "In a dream, silently, she had come to him, her wasted body within its loose graveclothes giving off an odour of wax and rosewood, her breath bent over him with mute secret words, a faint odour of wetted ashes." Richard Kain has pointed out the recurrence of this image in the "Nestor" episode (as Stephen helps a slow pupil with his algebra), in the "Proteus" episode (passive), in the library scene while he is meditating on *Hamlet*, and in the "Circe" episode where Stephen's mother appears in her "loose graveclothes."

These images of Stephen's mother on her deathbed or in her death clothes are the thematic bases for the most emotionally charged monologues in the novel. There are many more image-motifs, however, mostly associated with Leopold Bloom. One of the most pathetic, if humorous, of these is Leopold's many visions of Molly at the time he courted her. The thematic function of this motif is to show Leopold's yearning love for Molly, despite his

quiet acceptance of her lovers and his own clumsy phi-
landering.

The symbol-motif is even more often exploited in
Ulysses. The most amusing example of this is the baked
potato which Leopold Bloom carries with him. It is a
talisman for Leopold, "a relic of poor mama" as he tells
the prostitute in the brothel scene (p. 542); and earlier
(p. 488) it is referred to as "a Potato Preservative against
Plague and Pestilence." Whenever Bloom reaches in his
pocket to make sure the talisman is with him, it is an in-
dication he is setting forth on heroic ventures. Such a
venture is his trip to the butcher shop. Or it may indicate
that he is in great distress as it does when he is confused
by the probability of running into his rival, Blazes Boy-
lan. Bloom's monologue in that situation follows:

> Look for something I.
>
> His hasty hand went quick into a pocket, took
> out, read unfolded Agendath Netaim. Where did
> I?
>
> Busy looking for.
>
> He thrust back quickly Agendath.
>
> Afternoon she said.
>
> I am looking for that. Yes, that. Try all pockets.
> Handker. Freeman. Where did I? Ah, yes. Trou-
> sers. Purse. Potato. Where did I?
>
> Hurry. Walk quietly. Moment more. My heart.
>
> His hand looking for the where did I put found
> in his hip pocket soap lotion have to call tepid paper
> stuck. Ah soap there! Yes. Gate.
>
> Safe! [P. 181.]

Bloom's confusion is indicated by the staccato monologue and the furious search for a familiar object on his
person. The potato, his "preservative against pestilence"
is one of the things he finds. The other two objects, the
Zionist brochure *Agendath Netaim* and the bar of soap
are similar symbol-motifs in *Ulysses.* All of these articles
serve as significantly trivial counterparts to the protec-
tive gods in Homer's *Odyssey.* The symbolic function of

these objects is heightened in the "Circe" episode where they take on personification as characters in that hysterical drama, just as the Homeric gods enter the scene with mortal attributes in times of crisis in the *Odyssey*.

The employment of words and phrases as a special type of symbol-motif is a device at which Joyce is adept. It is worth digressing here to note what has so often been noted by other writers on Joyce, that if there is one aspect of his art which distinguishes him from any other novelist, it is his concentration on and sensitivity to language for its own sake. He is concerned with the individual word in particular. Harry Levin, for example, points out that the autobiographical Stephen of the *Portrait* was "a lyrical youth trying his magic by attaching phrases to feelings," and that "Joyce with his highly developed auditory imagination and his unhappy estrangement from society, came to equate language and experience."[4] Frederick Hoffman says, "The odyssey of Bloom rests upon tenuous and accidental combinations of words."[5] In *Finnegans Wake*, Joyce exhibits the utmost concern over the power of the single word or phrase. It is this same kind of concern which lies back of the frequent use of the word-motif in *Ulysses*.

Such a motif is, for example, the famous "met him pike hoses," which represents Molly Bloom's attempt to pronounce "metempsychosis." It first appears in the "Calypso" episode when Molly asks Leopold what the word means. Bloom thinks of it again later in the same episode and again in the "Sirens" episode; it reappears in his mind in the "Nausicaä" episode, in the "Oxen of the Sun" scene, and finally in the "Circe" drama. The meaning it evokes is always that of reincarnation—a concept Leopold is concerned with very seriously. The theme of reincarnation and regeneration is an important one in the book. For this reason, reappearance of the "big word" which bothers Molly recurs with the power of a motif. The theme is accented by its appearance in other ways in the monologue of Stephen, Leopold, and

Molly. It is also a corollary to the idea of the Viconian Cycle which interested Joyce. In a similar manner, many other word- and phrase-motifs are used in *Ulysses*. Such are "omphalos," "La ci darem . . . ," "sweets of sin"; these and many more are listed according to their appearances in *Ulysses* in an appendix to Kain's *Fabulous Voyager*. All of the motifs are signals to the reader to watch for thematic material that otherwise, in the vagaries of this world of prespeech consciousness, might be lost or obscured.[6]

The most overt pattern Joyce follows in *Ulysses* is, of course, that of the burlesque (or parody) of Homer's *Odyssey*. It is conclusively established that Joyce did this deliberately and carefully. It is certain that his three main characters are patterned, in burlesque fashion, after the three main characters of the *Odyssey;* and that his novel is, like the epic, divided into three main parts: the "Telemechia," "The Voyage," and the "Nostos"; and that the episodes follow those of the *Odyssey*, although Joyce rearranges them.[7]

The only specific key to this pattern in the book itself is in its title. There are innumerable suggestions of it, however, throughout the work. Gilbert's book on Joyce is indispensable for following the Homeric pattern in *Ulysses*. Gilbert's work is able to carry the weight of authority because Joyce approved of it before its publication and even aided Gilbert in planning it.

It is not necessary, then, to explain the Homeric parallel in *Ulysses* here, since it has been done so thoroughly elsewhere. The point of interest to us is to determine how this particular pattern influences Joyce's stream-of-consciousness novel. From the *Odyssey*, Joyce works in three directions in order to provide unity to his novel: first, he uses the themes of the narrative itself, reducing them to burlesque proportions; second, he employs the symbolic structure of the *Odyssey* and uses Homeric images and symbols; and third, he follows the episodical or scenic arrangement of the *Odyssey*. Because of the close-knit quality of these three types of pattern as Joyce uses them, it is profitable to consider them together. It must be pointed out, however, that the first two of these, the burlesque epic and the symbolic structure, function not only as patterns but also as specific keys to character interpretation.

The epic quality of *Ulysses* is adhered to in the opening invocation, although it is a mockery; it is found in the use of flash-backs equivalent to the epic device of *in medias res;* it is carried through in its concentration on a single hero, Leopold Bloom; it carries this hero through a series of adventures; it is written (usually) in mock-grand style; and it carries a cosmic overview (e.g., Molly as Gaea-Tellus). The themes of the narrative itself also reflect the epic model of the *Odyssey.* These themes, more than anything else, add meaning and give direction to the materials in the consciousness of Stephen-Telemachus, Leopold-Ulysses, and Molly-Penelope. An illustration is useful to indicate the manner and the importance of this.

Let us consider the "Lestrygonian" episode, named after the cannibalistic race which Ulysses and his men encountered. The cannibals' activities in Homer's epic are serious and the scene is brief and dramatically tense.[8] In Joyce's mock epic, the crisis involves simply Bloom's difficulties in finding a place to eat lunch. Both scenes, however, have to do primarily with food. The episode in *Ulysses* opens with Leopold Bloom's consciousness flowing:

> Pineapple rock, lemon platt, butter scotch. A sugar-sticky girl shovelling scoopfuls of creams for a christian brother. Some school treat. Bad for their tummies. Lozenges and comfit manufacturer to His Majesty the King. God. Save. Our. Sitting on his throne sucking red jujubes white. [P. 149.]

In like manner, terms referring to food and the digestive processes permeate the remaining part of the episode.

Bloom, then, is hungry and he is searching for a place

to eat lunch. The land of the Lestrygonians has its counterpart in Dublin. This is a cheap and foul restaurant where Bloom-Ulysses reacts in disgust to the "animals feeding"; which is, on a different level, suggestive of the horror of Odysseus when the cannibals snatch his men for their dinner. Bloom's disgust colors his thoughts: "Smells of men. His gorge rose. Spaton sawdust, sweetish warmish cigarette smoke, reek of plug, spilt beer, men's beery piss, the stale of ferment." (P. 167.)

Gilbert points out numerous direct recalls in this chapter of *Ulysses* to the disaster of Odysseus and his men at Lamos. He comments, for example, on the scene in which Leopold stops to feed the gulls with some buns:

> "The gulls swooped silently two, then all, from their heights, pouncing on prey. Gone. Every morsel. Aware of their greed and cunning, he shook the powdery crumb from his hands. They never expected that." Mr. Bloom pictures a communal kitchen with a "soup pot as big as the Phoenix Park. Harpooning flitches and hindquarters out of it." The descent of the gulls, pouncing on prey, recalls the onslaught of the Lestrygonians, swooping down from their cliffs on the unexpected quarry, and the soup pot may be likened to the ring of the harbour, where the crews of all the Achaean ships save that of Odysseus (who had prudently moored without) were drowned or harpooned by the cannibals.
>
> The callous King Antiphates is symbolized by Mr. Bloom's imperious hunger; the sight and reek of food are the decoy, his daughter, and the horde of the Lestrygonians may be likened to the teeth. . . .[9]

Although this interpretation on analogical grounds becomes almost absurd as Gilbert carries it through to the last paragraph quoted above, it clearly reveals to what extent and in what manner Bloom's character comes out in this episode; and it is because of the epic background and not because of any sustained action. The point is that the theme and situation, determined as they are by their counterparts in the *Odyssey*, serve only to give a framework to carry on the chief function of the book: the depiction of psychological character. A clear illustration of this comes from consideration of the secondary theme of the episode, a theme that is found both in the *Odyssey* and in *Ulysses*. We have Joyce's own word (quoted by Frank Budgen) for the significance of the parallel:

> "I am now writing the Lestrygonians episode, which corresponds to the adventure of Ulysses with the cannibals. My hero is going to lunch. But there is a seduction motive in the *Odyssey*, the cannibal king's daughter. Seduction appears in my book as women's silk petticoats hanging in a shop window. The words through which I express the effect of it on my hungry hero are: 'Perfume of embraces all him assailed. With hungered flesh obscurely, he mutely craved to adore.'"[10]

Something of this burlesque reference to Homer's themes and situations is found in every episode of *Ulysses*. With it comes a point from which to interpret Joyce's purpose. There is nothing heroic in this Dublin land of Leopold's wanderings. The age of Bloom-Ulysses is, according to Joyce, an age of small issues.

Joyce's aims were complex and he wanted to say very much; fortunately he was able to do this, for there are almost no limits to his talents for manufacturing unifying devices. Some of these, however, add little to his basic purposes. Such is the celebrated thematic organization of the episodes of *Ulysses* according to human anatomy, art, color, technique, and symbol. Stuart Gilbert offers the key to this as he does to the more important Homeric parallel.[11] For example, the "Hades" episode, which has to do with Bloom's attending the funeral and burial of his friend Patrick Dignam, has as its anatomical theme, the heart; as its art theme, religion; as its color theme, white and black; as its technique, "incubism"; and as its symbol, the caretaker. In like manner, each of the episodes has a specific organ, art, color, technique, and symbol theme of its own fastened onto the main framework of the *Odyssey* burlesque. The purpose of this is to give greater unity to the whole so that the unities in *Ulysses* become "as manifold and withal symmetrical as the daedal network of nerves and blood-streams which pervade the living organism."[12] One feels that in all this straining after symmetry there is an unprofitable overcomplication. At times, even, there are negative results when the materials of the narrative are forced into patterns which function only for the sake of the pattern itself. Such is, I believe, the "embryonic development" technique of the fourteenth ("Oxen of the Sun") episode. It would be as well to label the technique there "parody," for the episode is written in a manner which parodies English style from that of unidentified early Anglo-Saxon to a twentieth-century American evangelist's polemics. It includes parodies of Mandeville, Malory, Browne, Bunyan, Pepys, Swift, Sterne, Goldsmith, Gibbon, Lamb, de Quincey, Landor, Dickens, Newman, Pater, Ruskin, and Carlyle. This is done brilliantly, and the pertinence of the "embryonic technique" to the dominating theme of birth is obvious. But it is out of proportion to its function; and the interweaving of birth, embryonic growth, the art of medicine, and literary travesty makes crude motley.

Some of the times, however, these secondary unities give necessary focus for the contents of a character's psyche. Such is the case in the "Lestrygonian" episode noted earlier in this chapter. Here, the "peristaltic" technique and the theme of the digestive organs are closely related to the Homeric episode; all of which, when it is set against the essential fact that Bloom is hungry and wants to eat lunch, is not only particularly relevant, but also gives clarity and credence to the concentration of Bloom's psyche on food and eating.

There are still other devices for gaining symmetry which Joyce employs in *Ulysses*. Two of these involve utilization of theoretical cyclic schemes. One is the Viconian theory of historical cycles; the other is the sonata form of music. The utilization of the Viconian Cycle is more important because it is a possible explanation of why Joyce rearranged the Homeric episodes as he did. The active interest Joyce had in the historical theories of the Italian scholar, Giambattista Vico, is well known. Commentators on *Finnegans Wake* have explained the influence Vico's Cycle had on that work, and more recently it has been determined that such an influence is found in *Ulysses*.[13] The suggestion is reasonable and the evidence is convincing. The advantage of this pattern is that, unlike the Homeric pattern, it is not limited to any given time or place. Thus the functions of the characters in *Ulysses* can be so ordered as to give them greater significance to the modern world. They take from their adherence to Viconian types symbolic values which are more directly universal than those the Homeric symbolic values suggest.

The idea of musical structure in *Ulysses* is so general that it is not very important, although it is interesting always to observe Joyce's unusual resources. It is Ezra Pound who described *Ulysses* as a musical sonata form with a theme, a counter-theme, meeting, development and finale.[14] Fortunately, Pound's point loses little of its force, despite the fact that what he describes is not entirely accurate for the sonata form. Professor Beach has also made a musical analogy in referring to the structure of *Ulysses*. He writes, "*Ulysses* is nothing more nor less than a symphonic poem, characterized by a vigorous and insistent development of themes." [15] Although analogies from one art technique to another are easily misleading, these general descriptions of the musical structure of *Ulysses* are valid.

Virginia Woolf's Symbolic Design

If one wished to compare the structure of a novel to a sonata form, *Mrs. Dalloway* would serve as a superb example. It is easy to identify there a first theme, a bridge passage, a second theme, development, and recapitulation. In Virginia Woolf's novels, however, as in Joyce's, more tangible patterns are employed to provide harmony.

Virginia Woolf does much the same thing with the unities in *Mrs. Dalloway* as Joyce does with them in *Ulysses*. The surface narrative of *Mrs. Dalloway* takes place within twenty-four hours; it takes place in the city of London (and in one district of that city); and it involves two major characters. Yet the time involved in the basic drama which takes place within the minds of these characters covers eighteen years; the place of incident varies from India to Bourton to London to the World War battlefields of France; and about a dozen characters are involved. The unities in *Mrs. Dalloway*, amazing as they are in their strictness, are superimposed on a narrative which greatly lacks them. The function of this dualism is the same as it is in *Ulysses*: it makes it possible for an outside consciousness (the reader's) to follow, understand, and interpret the minds of the characters which the author creates. This is managed, as it is in *Ulysses*, by providing a fairly static focal point for the reader's attention to return to while he is following the helter-skelter associations of the characters' consciousnesses.

Virginia Woolf also makes some use of motifs as unifying devices. Such is the sound image in *Mrs. Dalloway* of Big Ben striking the hours of the day; such also is the recurring symbol of the lighthouse in *To the Lighthouse*. Virginia Woolf's reliance on symbols as structural patterns is, however, most emphatic in a different sense. Especially is this true in *To the Lighthouse*, where the entire novel is based on a set of primary symbolic values. It is true to a great extent in *The Waves* and to some extent in *Mrs. Dalloway*. An examination of *To the Lighthouse* will reveal the manner in which this symbolic structure functions to give the needed coherency of pattern in stream-of-consciousness fiction.

As the title implies, the substance of the novel is the attempt of the characters to get to the lighthouse, which is on an island a few miles from where they are gathered. The book opens with this emphasized: " 'Yes, of course, if it's fine tomorrow,' said Mrs. Ramsay. 'But you'll have to be up with the lark,' she added." Mrs. Ramsay is telling her son, James, that he can go to the lighthouse if the weather will permit it. The book closes, after ten years have passed and Mrs. Ramsay is dead, with James finally, and for the first time, arriving at the lighthouse. Of course, this is not an adventure story, and the novel is not taken up with boat wrecks and storms and the like. The lighthouse is a symbol, just as the setting of the novel, the isolated island in the Hebrides, is used symbolically, and just as the characters and their actions are symbolic. Indeed, as it has been suggested, the lighthouse symbol penetrates the novel with uncircumscribed power: "The structure of the book itself reproduces the effect of the lighthouse beam, the long flash represented by the first movement (The Window) [that is, the first division of the book], the interval of darkness represented by the second movement (Time Passes) and the second and shorter flash by the last movement (The Lighthouse). When this aspect of the book is thought of the subject is no longer a particular group of human beings; it is life and death, joy and pain—more specifically two themes stand out, the isolation of the individual human spirit and the contrast between the disordered and fragmentary experience of living and the ideal truth or beauty to which the human mind aspires."[16]

Mrs. Ramsay, the champion of the trip to the lighthouse, is opposed by her husband, who answers her opening remarks: " 'But,' said his father, stopping in front of the drawing room window, 'it won't be fine.' " Thus the basic situation is infused with symbolic meaning in the opposing of two forces. The general relationships of the characters, the struggle after answers to basic problems of knowledge, the search for keys to memories and impressions take on the significance that comes with a mystical quest. It is, in Virginia Woolf, all a matter of insight, for the symbolic values cannot be defined; and when one finds them, one knows it only by intuition, by "sensing" it. David Daiches, who has explored this aspect of Virginia Woolf more thoroughly than anyone else, says of *To the Lighthouse:*

> Virginia Woolf passes from one consciousness to another, from one group to another, exploring the significance of their reactions, following the course of their meditations, carefully arranging and patterning the images that rise up in their minds, bringing together with care and economy, a select number of symbolic incidents, until a design has been achieved . . . and experience is seen as something inexpressible yet significant.[17]

It is, then, the significance of events and memories and associations that is pointed up by Virginia Woolf. She is aware that she cannot express their meanings. In order to impress the reader with the significance of going to the lighthouse, this subtle novelist employs another symbolic situation to serve as counterpoint to the basic one. This is centered on Lily Briscoe, one of the guests of the Ramsays, who throughout the ten years is trying to finish a landscape painting. She finishes it at the precise moment when James arrives at the lighthouse. Then she has, of a sudden, a moment of insight, of inspiration: "With a sudden intensity, as if she saw it clear for a second, she drew a line there, in the centre. It was done; it was finished. Yes, she thought, laying down her brush in extreme fatigue, I have had my vision."[18]

The symbolic design and the symbolic vision can be found in most of Virginia Woolf's work. Clarissa Dalloway's day, her preparations for the party, her final realization of herself at the party are symbolic. In this manner the trivial subject gains inexpressible significance, just as the trivial in consciousness gains meaning when it has symbolic reference. For example, Clarissa Dalloway is alone in her bedroom while her party is going on downstairs. She is looking out the window:

> —in the room opposite the old lady stared straight at her! She was going to bed. And the sky. It will be a solemn sky, she had thought, it will be a dusky sky, turning away its cheek in beauty. But there it was—ashen, pale, raced over quickly by tapering vast clouds. It was new to her. The wind must have risen. She was going to bed, in the room opposite. . . . She pulled the blind now. The clock began striking. The young man had killed himself; but she did not pity him; with the clock striking the hour, one, two, three, she did not pity him, with all this going on. There! the old lady had put out her light! the whole house was dark now with this going on, she repeated, and the words came to her, Fear no more the heat of the sun. She must go back to them. But what an extraordinary night! She felt somehow very like him—the young man who had killed himself. She felt glad he had done it; thrown it away.[19]

It is the symbolic, private meaning of all this which illuminates for Clarissa her actions and the actions of the humanity (the woman going to bed, the young man who killed himself) around her; and it is the symbolic significance which illuminates *for the reader* the meaning of the commonplace in the mind of Clarissa.

Although *The Waves* is also built on a broad symbolic pattern, the chief structural device Virginia Woolf uses in that novel is one of formal scenic arrangements. This is combined with the symbolic force of the rising and falling tides, the rising and setting sun, and the continuous advance of the waves on the shore. The scenic design is managed by the presentation of seven groups of stylized soliloquies which represent seven stages in the lives of the characters. Each group of soliloquies is introduced by a passage of poetic prose describing the advance of the tide on a seashore. These descriptions advance from sunrise to sunset as the characters advance in age from childhood to middle age. The introductory descriptions are symbolic. For example, the first one is a prelude to the stage of childhood when things are beginning for the characters:

> The sun had not yet risen. The sea was indistinguishable from the sky, except that the sea was slightly creased as if a cloth had wrinkles in it. Gradually the sky whitened, a dark line lay on the horizon dividing the sea from the sky and the grey cloth became barred with thick strokes moving, one after another, beneath the surface, following each other, pursuing each other perpetually.

The soliloquies of Bernard, Neville, Louis, Susan, Jinny, and Rhoda, children who live together, follow this. They reveal their innermost selves and their revelations are complemented by the thoughts of each one about the other five. The scene suddenly and arbitrarily changes. The new scene is introduced by another poetic description which again has symbolic meaning: "The sun rose higher. . . ." That is, the children are advancing in age, so it is appropriate for the scene of the next group of soliloquies to take place at the moment when the children are leaving for boarding schools. The book ends with a scene of reunion when the characters are past middle age, and there is a final one-sentence description of the seashore to close the story: "The waves broke on the shore."

The formal scenic arrangement of *The Waves* serves as a substitute for the lack of time unity and of plot, for each scene carries its own unity of time and the whole book is connected by the symbolic descriptions between the scenes. This great degree of formalization is in harmony with the stylized manner of the soliloquies.

Faulkner's Synthesis

An entirely different kind of scenic pattern is found in Faulkner's *As I Lay Dying*. This novel, like *The Waves*, is composed of a group of soliloquies. Like *The Waves* also, it is presented in a set of scenes unconnected by any objective narrative. But there the similarity ends. The arbitrarily presented scenes in *As I Lay Dying* are introduced simply by titles identifying the speaker, similar to such descriptions in plays. The soliloquies are not stylized in the manner of a writer's formal style with the same style for each of the characters as they are in *The Waves*. Instead, they are written in the idiom and thought patterns typical of each character. It may be summarily stated that Faulkner's use of formal arrangement of scenes in *As I Lay Dying* is a device for making it possible to introduce the thoughts of a great many characters without unduly confusing the reader. There are thirteen characters whose consciousnesses are represented in this short novel. This distinguishes it from all other stream-of-consciousness fiction, which varies in this respect from only one important character in *Pilgrimage* to six in *The Waves*.

Faulkner's chief unifying device in this novel is something else. It is a unity of action which he employs. In other words, he uses a substantial plot, the thing that is lacking in all other stream-of-consciousness literature. It is this differentiating aspect of Faulkner's work (the same thing is true in *The Sound and the Fury*) which we have noted twice before. It is the thing that carries *As I Lay Dying* and *The Sound and the Fury* away from the pure stream-of-consciousness type of novel to a point where the traditional novel and stream of consciousness are combined. Because there is a coherent plot and because the characters act in an external drama which has a beginning, complications, climax, and ending, the absolute need for further unifying devices does not exist. What is egocentric and chaotic, in, say, Darl's mind, can be understood because it has reference to a clearly built conflict and problem of action. For example, in the following passage, when Darl's consciousness is represented just after someone has asked him where his brother, Jewel, is, the content becomes clear to the reader on the basis of a brooding conflict between the two brothers:

> Down there fooling with that horse. He will go on through the barn, into the pasture. The horse will not be in sight: He is up there among the pine seedlings, in the cool. Jewel whistles, once and shrill. The horse snorts, then Jewel sees him, glinting for a gaudy instant among the blue shadows. Jewel whistles again; the horse comes dropping down the slope, stiff-legged, his ears cocking and flicking, his mis-matched eyes rolling, and fetches up twenty feet away, broadside on, watching Jewel over his shoulder in an attitude kittenish and alert.[20]

Usually in this novel, the contents of the characters' psyches are essentially observations of other characters. This offers a special problem for Faulkner, because in depending on the observational content of consciousness, he is forced to give less of the content which arises from the workings of memory and the imagination. Such selecting tends to make the representation of consciousness unconvincing. Faulkner partly circumvents this difficulty with two devices: first, he deals only with a fairly surface level of consciousness in *As I Lay Dying;* and second, he is faithful to the idiom and language which most accurately represents the particular character. Thus the effect of verisimilitude of consciousness is achieved.

As I Lay Dying is a fairly simple and unsubtle work compared to Faulkner's other stream-of-consciousness novel, *The Sound and the Fury.* These novels are, however, similar in several technical matters: both contain substantial unity of action, but that of the latter is more complex; both have a formal scenic arrangement, but that of the latter is at once more complex and less clear-cut. The technical similarity does not go much past this; for *The Sound and the Fury* deals with complex personalities, and consciousness is presented in it at an extremely deep level. Consequently, other structural devices are needed to clarify for the reader what is going on in this particular world of consciousness. The chief of these other devices are symbolic structure and motif. So what we have as patterns for unity in *The Sound and the Fury* are closely intertwined plot, unity of time, scenic arrangement, symbolic framework, and motifs. None of these is predominant in effectiveness and none is clear-cut.

The plot of *The Sound and the Fury* is presented in terms of the lives of the four children of the Compson family, a once respectable and proud Mississippi family that is in its last stages of decay. This process of decay is symbolized by the gradual vanishing of "The Compson domain," originally a choice square mile of land with its "slave quarters and stables and kitchen gardens and the formal lawns and promenades and pavilions laid out by the same architect who built the columned porticoed house furnished by steamboat from France and New Orleans. . . ." The process of decay is dramatized by the story of the destruction of the children, Benjy, Quentin III, Candace (Caddy), and Jason IV. Since the destruction, except with Jason, is an inner one, the drama presenting the destruction, except the part that deals with Jason, has as its setting the psyches of the characters.

The problems of time unity and of scenic arrangement are, of course, closely worked out in relation to this action unity or plot. It is complex. The first section of the novel is labeled "April 7, 1928." That is the date that stands for the "now" of this scene. The setting is the mind of the idiot, Benjy, who in 1928 is thirty-three years old, but whose mental age is three. Benjy's consciousness follows the same laws of movement and association that other consciousnesses do, except perhaps it moves with greater fluidity. Thus the "present" in his mind moves freely through the past years of his life, so that there is to his consciousness, more than to that of anyone else in fiction, a quality of flux. This section of the novel, then, has to be considered on two levels: that of the events of the day, April 7, 1928, and that of the past events in the life of Benjy. The events of the "present" concern what happens to Benjy and to his keeper, the Negro boy, Luster. The accomplishment on this level is presentation of a subtheme centered on the Negro-white relationship, a corollary to the main theme of Compson degeneracy. The materials of the past are the important ones here for purposes of plot. Benjy's psychic character is dramatized and the crucial past events and personages (especially Candace) in the Compson family history are presented from the point of view of the simple, but strangely lucid idiot. Faulkner tells us, "Benjy loved three things: The pasture which was sold to pay for Candace's wedding and to send Quentin to Harvard, his sister Candace, firelight."[21] Since Benjy's love is uniquely persistent and unwavering, these three things, and little else, form the materials of his consciousness. The narrative significance of this lies in the fact that the "pasture" is a metonymy for the vanishing Compson domain, the central symbol of the novel; "Candace" is the only one of the Compson children whose consciousness is not directly presented, so that she is dealt with as a character in this indirect way; and "firelight" is a vital symbol for the exceptional insight of the idiot. This insight gives the materials of Benjy's consciousness a certain weight of authority in relation to the whole novel, in spite of his idiocy. It is by this concentration on three basic subjects in Benjy's mind that not only is it possible for a reader to grasp what is going on, but it is also possible for him to become grounded in the materials of the plot.

The second episode of the novel is entitled "June 2, 1910." The external setting is Cambridge, Massachusetts, on the title date; the plot is concerned with Quentin's preparation for suicide. The internal setting is Quentin's mind, which, like Benjy's, flows freely in the past. The plot here is a supplement to the main plot of the novel, which was sketched in the opening section. Quentin, although he is intelligent, is extremely unstable psychologically, so that he, even more than Benjy, is obsessed; and, like Benjy, his sister Candace is the object of his obsession. Thus the development of Candace's character and her role in the broad scheme of things is again advanced. The brotherly concern, in this instance, is incestuous, but it is not physical; it is symbolic for Quentin, "who loved not his sister's body, but some concept of Compson honor."[22] The incestuous relation becomes a symbol itself related to the main plot and to the theme of the whole novel.

The third and the last sections are labeled "April 6, 1928," and "April 8, 1928," respectively, which, it will be noted, are the day before and the day after the opening episode. The primary method of the first of these sections is not internal monologue as was that of the two previous ones, but it is soliloquy on a surface, communicating level. It concerns the fourth and youngest of the Compson children, Jason IV. Because chiefly the surface narrative is unfolded here, the time element is fairly static. The same is true of the last section, except that an even more conventional method is used, that of the omniscient third person narrator. Jason's role in the drama of the degeneration of the Compson family is properly the last one treated because it is climactic; that is, his degeneration is the ultimate one. Although he is the only sane one of the brothers, his degeneracy is greater because it involves a break with Compson standards of integrity. Robert Penn Warren has noted this in his remarks on Faulkner. He says of Jason: ". . . there is no one who can be compared in degradation and vileness to Jason of *The Sound and the Fury*, the Compson who has embraced Snopesism. In fact, Popeye and Flem, Faulkner's best advertised villains, cannot, for vileness and ultimate meanness, touch Jason."[23]

Jason's conflict is with two persons (his father is dead

and so is his brother, Quentin, the two chief upholders of Compson honor): Dilsey, the old Negro cook who understands Compson honor, at least in its externals, and Miss Quentin, Candace's illegitimate daughter. Miss Quentin lives with the Compsons, but she doesn't understand (or care for) the Compson code. She represents a deliberate animality foreign to all Compsons—even to Jason. Jason's defeat is by Miss Quentin, not by Dilsey. Symbolically, the Compson line is ended with Jason's defeat (he leaves no heir), and Quentin's suicide (he never cohabits, except imaginatively and symbolically with his sister). Benjy, of course, is gelded and is finally committed to the State Asylum. This story parallels the defeat of the Sutpen dynasty in *Absalom, Absalom!*

It is by this complicated, but organic, use of plot, time unity, scenic arrangement, and symbolic frame that Faulkner achieves a pattern of structural unity in *The Sound and the Fury*. In addition, he makes interesting use of motifs to aid in the binding together of these other structural elements.

Faulkner's particular use of motifs can be found in either of the first two sections of the novel. It will be sufficient for illustration to examine but one of them. In the second episode, which contains Quentin's monologue, the motifs are chiefly symbol-motifs, although there are some image-motifs also. The word-motif is not used frequently by Faulkner, who does not, like Joyce, "equate words with things." The chief motifs are the watch, the wedding announcement, the pasture, the chimes, the images of tidying up, and the word "sister." In a previous chapter dealing with the privacy of associations, it was shown that these things reappear in Quentin's consciousness. They recur constantly as signals, not only to Quentin's mind, but to the reader's as well. These motifs carry the main weight of the plot, and they are the means by which universal and coherent meaning is distilled from private and chaotic meaning. For example, the watch, which often appears as an object of Quentin's attention, is the watch Quentin's father presented to him. Quentin denudes it of its hands in order to prove to himself that his father's theory is valid: that its purpose is "not that you may remember time, but that you might forget it now and then for a moment and not spend all your breath trying to conquer it." The click of the watch, which doesn't tell time but only tells that time is always passing, is emphasized by the various clocks—Quentin always refuses to look at them—that impinge on Quentin's consciousness. These watch and clock references support two important ideas related to the main theme: one is the disjuncture of consciousness while it is coping with psychological versus calendar time; the other is the more general idea of decay in time.

It is not necessary for our purpose to show the manner in which all of these motifs are used in the novel. One of them, however, is particularly instructive as an example of the manner of utilizing motif that is found generally throughout Faulkner's writing. This is the narrative imagery that has to do with Quentin's concern with his appearance before he commits suicide. He is depicted as washing his hands, cleaning his tie with gasoline, brushing his teeth, and brushing his hat, before he leaves his room finally to go to the river. Of course Faulkner has to have him doing something in order to give a focus to the processes of his consciousness. The symbolic value of this particular imagery, which because it recurs so frequently takes on the status of motif, is great. It may be considered the final and feeble act of cleaning up Compson disgrace and dishonor; a purgative attempt on Quentin's part to erase the stain Candace has put on his psyche. It comes as a preparation for the climax of the episode, the suicide itself, which is likewise an act of atonement.

At least one stream-of-consciousness writer is not concerned with such complex patterns as time and place unities, plot, symbolic structure, theoretical cycles, and burlesques. In fact, the only strong unifying principle that Dorothy Richardson uses in her long *Pilgrimage* is that of unity of character. And this she employs to what must be a limit of its possibilities. Everything in every volume of *Pilgrimage* is presented from the point of view of Miriam. Actually, this is sufficient pattern for this novel, partly because it stays on a fairly surface level of consciousness, and partly because Dorothy Richardson does not have many themes to get across. In fact, it is difficult to determine if there is any theme presented in *Pilgrimage*. The subject is obviously Miriam's rather uneventful life, chiefly her psychic life. It is possible that there is an underlying "quest" theme, a kind of mystical search for something vague which is symbolized by "a tiny little garden." This garden image-motif runs through *Pilgrimage*, but there is nothing substantial in the way of structure for a reader to apply it to.

In the matter of structural patterns, we have come a long way from the complex layers of devices in *Ulysses* to the single device of character unity in *Pilgrimage*. Joyce we admire more than Richardson as an artificer, just as *Ulysses* we value more than *Pilgrimage* as a work of art. The reason for this is related to the reason that patterns are necessary at all in stream-of-consciousness fiction. We can let Joyce himself give the answer:

> "It [art] awakens, or ought to awaken, or induces, or ought to induce, an aesthetic stasis, an ideal pity or an ideal terror, a stasis called forth, prolonged and at last dissolved by what I call the rhythm of beauty."
>
> "What is that exactly?" asked Lynch.
>
> "Rhythm," said Stephen, "is the first formal aesthetic relation of part to part in any aesthetic whole or of an aesthetic whole to its part or parts or of any part to the aesthetic whole of which it is a part."[24]

Or, to make the answer simpler, we might venture an epigram and say that the crutches are needed only when there is weight to carry.

5

The Results

> *Once reality has been disclosed to us in this particular way, we continue to see it in this shape.*
>
> ERNST CASSIRER

IT HAS BECOME apparent that there is a pattern of development within the stream-of-consciousness genre. From the earliest experiments with impressionistic rendering of the inner world, illustrated at its best in Virginia Woolf's *Mrs. Dalloway* and at its most extensive in Dorothy Richardson's *Pilgrimage*, through the extremely forceful presentation of psychic life in Joyce's *Ulysses*, to the culmination of experiment in *The Waves* and *Finnegans Wake*—which led to stream of consciousness *en fleur*, and obscurity—we have come to a subtle retrenchment in Faulkner's novels. Faulkner's work represents a return to the fundamental basis of fiction, the prominent use of significant external action, which he combines with stream of consciousness.

Into the Main Stream

The stream-of-consciousness novel has entered the main stream of fiction. To look back on the era of experimentation with a sigh of relief and a reluctant admission that the experimenting produced some of the major literature of the century is not to appreciate the entire significance of the movement. The tremendous result is this: stream-of-consciousness methods are, now, conventional methods; the vagaries of prespeech mental life are established twentieth-century forms; the devices for conveying private consciousness are ones which writers use confidently and readers accept without a murmur. Stream of consciousness as a method of character depiction is a newly admitted reality. Art has always attempted to express, to objectify the dynamic processes of our inner life. Now that "inner life" is a reality which we recognize as available to any consciousness, and now that techniques, devices, and forms have been established for conveying this reality, fictional art has come closer than ever before to achieving its purpose.

But the acceptance of the reality of inner life, of the prespeech levels of consciousness, as a proper subject of fiction is the significant thing for us to notice. If we look, at random, at the work of some of the most important mid-century writers, this acceptance becomes obvious. One might notice it (and accept it as a standard convention) in the fiction of Elizabeth Bowen, Graham Greene, Katherine Anne Porter, Robert Penn Warren, Delmore Schwartz, and Eudora Welty—to mention but a few, and to overlook entirely the vast amount of more ephemeral work in which unuttered consciousness is not only casually accepted as a legitimate subject, but is even *automatically* formed in the image of the great experimental stream-of-consciousness novels.

We shall need but a few examples from the work of the authors listed above to amplify these observations. Mr. Warren's *All the King's Men,* a superb novel and a relatively popular one, was published in 1946. This novel, to get to the heart of the matter and to overlook a great deal of its power, is fundamentally a study of moral development and ethical awakening in the central character, Jack Burden. Burden's story, of course, is contingent on parallel and contrasting moral changes in the other main characters. For these—Willie Stark and Ann Stanton, principally—the development is almost entirely realized through action. For Burden, it is realized chiefly as *psychic drama.* Much of the writing in the novel is focused on depicting this inner drama of consciousness. Warren's method here is naturalistic (that is, he uses symbols and concrete images) rather than impressionistic. Like Faulkner, he takes the dense and chaotic materials of the mind and through symbols and motifs objectifies them. It is through rhetoric that he maintains the texture of density and chaos.

Warren's method of projecting Burden's unspoken mental activities is, however, not an imitation of Faulkner; the suggestion of stream of consciousness in *All the King's Men* is disarmingly conventional. It is usually presented in the first person, and sometimes in the more objective second person. ("Going to bed in the late spring afternoon or just at the beginning of twilight, with those sounds in your ears, gives you a wonderful sense of peace." [P. 325.]) Warren avoids mechanical devices, syntactical aberrations, fragments, and logical obscurity. This avoidance reflects his dislike of the purely mechanical (the psychoanalytical and theoretical) aspects of mental functioning. Warren's interest is in spiritual struggle (growth or decay), which manifests itself dramatically in the unuttered confusion of the mind. He depends on rhetoric, symbols, and free association to represent this confusion. It is significant that both the ignoring of psychological theories of consciousness and the accepting of the basic description which these theories have given Warren's generation are present in his depiction of his character. A brief example from the novel will suggest Warren's method. The first-person point of view and the third-person narrative indicate the dual function of the passage. That is, the narrative is carried forward, but more important, the mental state of Burden, the narrator, is clearly given also.

> She had been there since Adam's funeral. She had gone down with the body, trailing the sun-glittering, expensive hearse in an undertaker's limousine. . . . I didn't see her as she sat in the rented limousine which moved at its decorous tor-

turer's pace the near-hundred miles, lifting the miles slowly off the concrete slab, slowly and fastidiously as though you were peeling an endless strip of skin off the live flesh. I didn't see her, but I know how she had been: erect, white in the face, the beautiful bones of her face showing under the taut flesh, her hands clenched in her lap. For that was the way she was when I saw her standing under the moss-garlanded oaks, looking absolutely alone despite the nurse and Katy Maynard and all the people—friends of the family, curiosity-seekers come to gloat and nudge, newspapermen, big-shot doctors from town and from Baltimore and Philadelphia—who stood there while shovels did their work.[1]

The first sentence of this quotation is narrative. The rest is the imaginative association Burden makes. The images indicate the obsessive state of his mind, the insistent lingering on an object (the picture of Ann). At the same time, the associations with other events, themes, and motifs in the novel are skillfully (and realistically) recalled.

A more obvious echo from stream of consciousness can be found throughout Warren's later novel, *World Enough and Time* (1950). It is interesting to observe that in this novel the impressionistic method of Virginia Woolf is reflected. Again, there are no signs of direct imitation or even of direct influence. The stream-of-consciousness texture of Warren's work appears as spontaneous and it is smoothly worked in with the basic method of his novel, the journal combined with the omniscient third-person narrative of external events. The following example comes immediately after a description of the character, Jeremiah, as he is peering in the window of a friend's house. From the description of external events, the narration flows into a description of Jeremiah's consciousness. The italics are Warren's.

So that was Fort's wife, he thought. He had

known that she existed, but he had never seen her, she had not been real. But now she was real, and for an instant he felt some shift in the center of his intention, . . . and he strained to make out the words she was speaking but could hear nothing. Then he thought: *She doesn't love him, I can see from her face that she does not.* And thought with a sickening fear: *but if she did, if she did love him, could I . . . ?* And could not finish the notion, even in his mind, and with a leap of release, and sudden certainty, thought: *but she does not.* She could not, not with that face and that dead gaze upon him.[2]

This combination of omniscient description with internal monologue will recall to the reader the method used in *Mrs. Dalloway* and *To the Lighthouse*.

As a final example of the pervading influence of the stream-of-consciousness genre on recent fiction, notice of Katherine Anne Porter's *Pale Horse, Pale Rider* (1939) is illuminating. The particular interest here is the reflection, in a very lucid and otherwise conventionally managed story, of James Joyce's most radical technical innovations in *Ulysses*. I refer to the use of elaborate symbolism to express the dream qualities of consciousness. In Miss Porter's novelette, the reader is introduced, with an extremely effective montage of symbols, to the dream life of the character, Miranda. Later, in the story, the dream-fantasy, with all of its incoherency and disjointedness, is used in the representation of Miranda's fevered battle with death.

These more recent novels, influenced as their authors were by Woolf, Joyce, and Faulkner, are not stream-of-consciousness novels. The genre has been absorbed for the most part into the greater body of fictional method. The depiction of mental life in Mr. Warren's and Miss Porter's fiction (and in that of many other novelists as well) is similar to the psychological probing to be found in such pre-stream-of-consciousness novels as those by Henry James and Marcel Proust. But there is an important difference: James's and Proust's fiction was either obscure, or esoteric, or shockingly new, but the more recent novels are immediately available to a fairly wide reading public without the barriers of obscurity or strangeness present. Stream of consciousness had come between Henry James and Robert Penn Warren.

The intellectual interests and social forces which engendered and encouraged the stream-of-consciousness writers had intervened also. Consequently, when, in 1932, Professor Beach saw stream of consciousness as limited in its future by its invariable application to "neurotics," he was dismissing it altogether too soon. But when Professor Hoffman, twenty years later, regards the subject of stream-of-consciousness fiction as a "historically interesting" phase of novelistic method, corollary to popular interest in Freudian approaches to sex life, he is ignoring the results (and to some degree the achievements) of this phase. Both Professor Beach's and Professor Hoffman's errors are those of misplaced emphasis.[3] The aspects of stream-of-consciousness literature which emphasize the neurotic and Freudian sex life are not what distinguish it. One might argue, for example, that the characters in *Ulysses* and *To the Lighthouse* are no more—possibly much less—"neurotic" than are those in *The American Tragedy, Point Counter Point,* and *The Sun Also Rises,* to say nothing of those in *Antic Hay* and *Sanctuary.* Nor is the historical reflection of popular Freudianism more apparent in *Mrs. Dalloway* and *Pilgrimage* than it is in *Sons and Lovers* and *The Great Gatsby.* What has happened is this: when personality is examined as closely and candidly as it has been in the twentieth-century novel—in and out of stream of consciousness—it appears as an individual and not as a "norm." And if we have not been convinced in this century that everyone is abnormal, that the so-called neurotic condition is the general condition, we have learned nothing essential about ourselves at all. The stream-of-consciousness novel has given us empirical evidence for this truth. It has given us evidence of the metempirical also. We have learned from the explorers of man's psyche that the individual attempts, and sometimes achieves, a transcendency of what Balzac depicted as the *condition humaine*. The empirical world produces the neurotic personality; but that personality is able to yearn for contact with what is stable, for knowledge of the center of meaning. It is, then, with the overwhelming trend in fiction of our time to investigate meaning in human personality rather than in social action and reaction that stream of consciousness is allied. Representing an extreme concentration on unuttered consciousness, it produced its landmarks, towering ones, but it was subsumed by something basic in the nature of fiction: the need for surface action and external reality to make whole reality as man knows it, for man, as Joyce has illustrated, is only half-aspiring.

Summary

The new dimension in literature which the major stream-of-consciousness writers have created has been attempted before; it was attempted by the stream-of-consciousness writers themselves in non-stream-of-consciousness works. The special sense of immanent vision in *Mrs. Dalloway* and *To the Lighthouse* was suggested by Virginia Woolf in the earlier *Jacob's Room* and in the later *The Years*, but only when she used the basic techniques of stream of consciousness could she communicate it. Likewise, Joyce's satiric-pathetic comedy of existence was asserted in the stories in *Dubliners*, but it was wholly communicated only in the stream of consciousness of *Ulysses*. And Faulkner's sense of ironic tragedy, though powerful often in such novels as *Sanctuary* and *The Hamlet*, reaches the credibility necessary for the sharpest effectiveness only in his stream-of-consciousness works in which psychic drama prevails over grandiose rhetoric.

The basic techniques for presenting consciousness in literature are not inventions of the twentieth century. Both direct and indirect interior monologue can be found in works from previous centuries, and omniscient description and soliloquy were primary features of fiction even in its embryonic stages. The unique employment of these which produced stream of consciousness came with the twentieth-century novelists' awareness of the significance of the drama which takes place within the confines of the individual's consciousness.

There are two aspects of this drama of consciousness which posed particularly difficult problems for the writers who wanted to represent it. Among the philosopher-psychologists, William James and Henri Bergson convinced the following generations that consciousness flows like a stream and that the mind has its own time and space values apart from the arbitrary and set ones of the external world. Thus, flux and *durée* are aspects of psychic life for which new methods of narration had to be developed if writers were to depict them. The other aspect was more obvious: the mind is a private thing. The problem this posed was simply how could what is private be made public and still seem to have the qualities of privacy?

The chief device the writers hit upon for depicting and controlling both the movement and the privacy of consciousness was the utilization of the principles of mental free association. These provided a workable basis for imposing a special logic on the erratic meanderings of consciousness; thereby giving the writer a system to follow and the reader a system to hold on to. The process of free association further proved to be applicable to any particular consciousness in such a way as to show a pattern of association that depended on the individual's past experiences and his present obsessions. In this manner, the privacy problem was more than half solved.

But additional devices were needed to convey the unconventional movement and the enigma of privacy on the prespeech levels of consciousness. The ingenious minds of the writers we have been considering, like their contemporaries in the sister arts, especially in the cinema, found techniques which were devised to project the duality and the flux of mental life. Montage, with its function of presenting either more than one object or more than one time simultaneously, was especially adaptable to fiction. The corollary devices of "flashback," "fade-out," and "slow-up" proved useful adjuncts to montage and free association. Literary tradition itself was rummaged for devices and yielded such readymade materials as classical rhetoric and poetry could offer, including the particularly useful ones of metaphor and symbol. Even the conventions of punctuation were reshaped to produce the qualities of prespeech consciousness in words. The difficult job was finally accomplished, but where was the form of art in this?

Consciousness is in its prespeech levels unpatterned; a consciousness by its nature exists independent of action. In short, plot had to go by the wayside. Yet some kind of pattern had to be superimposed on the chaotic materials of consciousness. In lieu of a well-made plot, the writers devised all sorts of unities. They managed the closest adherence to the classical unities that the novel had ever produced; they patterned their work after literary models, historical cycles, and musical structure; they used complex symbolic structure, and finally they even managed to fuse external plot with stream of consciousness!

The Sound and the Fury and *As I Lay Dying*, latecomers in the stream-of-consciousness genre, are not pure examples of it. They contain an important element of plot, and they represent the point in the development of the twentieth-century novel at which stream of consciousness entered the main stream of fiction. It is still there, and the sacred waters of that stream are more potent than they were.

NOTES

Notes

CHAPTER 1.

¹ In *The Principles of Psychology* (New York, Henry Holt, 1890), I, 239.

² At least two writers, Frederick Hoffman and Harry Levin, have recognized this loose use of "stream of consciousness." Levin employs in its place the French rhetorical term *monologue intérieur*. Although Levin uses even this term too loosely for any general discussion of that technique, it serves well for his special purposes. I am indebted to him for the basic distinction between the terms in question. See his book, *James Joyce: A Critical Introduction* (Norfolk, Conn., New Directions, 1941), p. 89.

³ James Grier Miller, *Unconsciousness* (New York, J. Wiley and Sons, 1942), p. 18.

⁴ See the dictionaries of philosophy, particularly *Philosophisches Wörterbuch*, ed. Heinrich Schmidt, 10th ed. (Stuttgart, A. Kröner, 1943), and *The Dictionary of Philosophy*, ed. D. D. Runes (New York, The Philosophical Library, 1942). See also Frederick J. Hoffman's classification of stream-of-consciousness techniques according to four levels of consciousness in *Freudianism and the Literary Mind* (Baton Rouge, La., Louisiana State Univeristy Press, 1945), pp. 126–129.

⁵ For example: Edward Wagenknecht, *Cavalcade of the English Novel from Elizabeth to George VI* (New York, Henry Holt, 1943), p. 505.

⁶ It is, of course, true that there are several attempts to represent character in fiction in psychoanalytical terms—notably in Conrad Aiken's novels, *Blue Voyage* and *The Great Circle*—but these attempts are for the most part curiosities, and they are finally insignificant.

⁷ *The Principles of Psychology*, I, 239.

⁸ "Art of Fiction," *Partial Portraits* (London, Macmillan, 1905), p. 388.

⁹ *Pilgrimage*, 4 vols. (New York, Alfred A. Knopf, 1938), I, 10.

¹⁰ In *Dorothy M. Richardson* (London, Joiner and Steele, 1931), pp. 8 ff.

¹¹ *The Twentieth Century Novel: Studies in Technique* (New York, D. Appleton–Century, 1932), pp. 393 ff.

¹² Foreword to *Pilgrimage*, p. 10.

¹³ I refer particularly to the following: David Daiches, *Virginia Woolf* (Norfolk, Conn., New Directions, 1942); Bernard Blackstone, *Virginia Woolf: A Commentary* (London, Hogarth Press, 1949); and E. M. Forster, *Virginia Woolf* (New York, Harcourt, Brace, 1942).

¹⁴ "Modern Fiction," *The Common Reader* (New York, Harcourt, Brace, 1925), p. 212. Other essays in which Virginia Woolf expresses her ideas of reality and the novel are: "How It Strikes a Contemporary," in *The Common Reader; Mr. Bennett and Mrs. Brown* (New York, Harcourt, Brace, 1924); and *A Room of One's Own* (New York, Harcourt, Brace, 1929).

¹⁵ *Viking Portable Joyce* (New York, 1947), p. 481.

¹⁶ Richard Kain, of the commentators on *Ulysses*, treats the satiric cast of the novel with the most understanding: *Fabulous Voyager* (Chicago, University of Chicago Press, 1947), chaps. i and xv.

¹⁷ Ruel E. Foster, "Dream as Symbolic Act in Faulkner," *Perspective*, II (1949).

¹⁸ Sumner C. Powell, "William Faulkner Celebrates Easter, 1928," *Perspective*, II (1949).

¹⁹ George Marion O'Donnell in a remarkably seminal, if cursory, analysis of Faulkner's work ("Faulkner's Mythology," *Kenyon Review*, I, 1939) establishes this principle of interpretation. It is elaborated by Malcolm Cowley in the introduction to the *Viking Portable Faulkner* (New York, 1946). It is further modified by Robert Penn Warren in two essays that first appeared in *The New Republic* (1946); they are reprinted in *Forms of Modern Fiction*, ed. William Van O'Connor (Minneapolis, University of Minnesota Press, 1948).

CHAPTER 2.

¹ *Le monologue intérieur, son apparition, ses origines, sa place dans l'oeuvre de James Joyce* (Paris, A. Messein, 1931), tr. from pp. 58–59.

² Modern Library Edition (New York, Random House, 1934), p. 723. Subsequent references will be to this edition.

³ Actually, it is difficult to determine whether Aiken is really depicting his character in an actual dream state in that one section in which the consciousness of his protagonist, Andy, is extremely incoherent, or whether it is a waking reverie similar to Molly Bloom's monologue in *Ulysses*. There is no doubt that Joyce's object in *Finnegans Wake* is to depict the dream state. The dream mechanism with which this is done is based on a combination of Jung's theory of a collective consciousness (H. C. Earwicker's dream consciousness extends to realms far beyond Earwicker's experience) and Freudian theories of unconscious wit, verbal distortions, personality displacements, and the like. This Freudian mechanism for depicting direct interior monologue is analyzed thoroughly by Frederick Hoffman. The following from Hoffman's study (*Freudianism and the Literary Mind*) may be informative to an understanding of how special stream of consciousness can become:

"The purpose of *Finnegans Wake* is clearly to render dream-life into words. The linguistic habits of the dream-life, united under the terms *condensation* and *displacement*, are all abundantly revealed in Joyce's work. . . . Puns and portmanteau words are not strangers to the dream as Freud has abundantly shown; they constitute one of Joyce's chief devices: 'And of course all chimed *din width* the *eatmost* boviality,' and '*Eins* within a *space* and a *wearywide* space it *wast ere wohned* a Mookse.' [Italics Hoffman's.] . . . The dream, incapable of accommodating abstractions, converts *in medias res* into 'in midias reeds'; in another instance it uses the same devices to convert a religious line (the first line of the *Confiteor*) into a disguised sexual reference:

mea culpa mea culpa

May he colp, may colp her,

mea maxima culpa

may he mixandmass colp her!"

⁴ *Le monologue intérieur*, pp. 39–40.

⁵ In *The Common Reader* (New York, Harcourt, Brace, 1925), p. 213.

⁶ Such seekers after reader-confidence and verisimilitude as Defoe and Poe are recalled, so that we are reminded that the exit of the author is by no means confined to the twentieth century. See Edward Wagenknecht, *A Cavalcade of the English Novel from Elizabeth to George VI* (New York, Henry Holt, 1943) and Joseph Warren Beach, *The Twentieth Century Novel: Studies in Technique* (New York, D. Appleton–Century, 1932).

⁷ The reader may wonder, then, why Henry James is not considered here among stream-of-consciousness writers, because it is obviously true that James is frequently concerned with description of mental content. The salient thing that differentiates him from the stream-of-consciousness writers is the fact that he describes the rational weighing of intelligence; hence, he is concerned with consciousness on a level which corresponds to the speech level. It lacks the free-flowing, elliptic, and symbolic quality of true stream of consciousness.

⁸ *Pilgrimage* (New York, Alfred A. Knopf, 1938), I, 194–195.

⁹ Modern Library Edition (New York, Random House, 1930), p. 347.

¹⁰ *James Joyce: A Critical Introduction* (Norfolk, Conn., New Directions, 1941), p. 108.

¹¹ *The Twentieth Century Novel*, p. 497.

¹² *Rahab* (New York, Boni and Liveright, 1922), p. 213.

¹³ The first novelist to exploit this principle of psychic functioning was eighteenth-century Laurence Sterne, who has only slightly been outdone today, even by Joyce. But Sterne is not within the stream-of-consciousness genre because his concerns are not serious in representing psychic content for its own sake and as a means for achieving essences of characterization. His aims are broad rather than deep, hence his use of association is whimsical and, despite its probable influence on the moderns, is not the same as that of the writers under consideration here.

¹⁴ Joseph Campbell in "Finnegan the Wake," *James Joyce: Two Decades of Criticism*, ed. Seon Givens (New York, Viking, 1948), p. 371.

¹⁵ For comment on cinematic devices in literature, see Beach, *The Twentieth Century Novel*, Part V, and Sergei M. Eisenstein, *The Film Sense*, tr. Jay Leyda (New York, Harcourt, Brace, 1942), *passim*.

¹⁶ David Daiches, *Virginia Woolf* (Norfolk, Conn., New Directions, 1942), pp. 66 ff.

¹⁷ *Film Form*, ed. and tr. Jay Leyda (New York, Harcourt, Brace, 1949), p. 104.

[18] *James Joyce's Ulysses* (New York, Alfred A. Knopf, 1934), pp. 209 ff. Most of us who write on *Ulysses* are indebted greatly to Gilbert's pioneering work.

[19] *Fabulous Voyager* (Chicago, University of Chicago Press, 1947), pp. 277 ff.

[20] Modern Library Edition (New York, Random House, 1928; copyright 1925 by Harcourt, Brace), pp. 29 ff.

[21] Modern Library Edition (New York, Random House, 1929), p. 24.

[22] (New York, Harcourt, Brace, 1927), p. 159.

CHAPTER 3.

[1] Modern Library Edition, p. 422.

[2] *Ibid.*, p. 192.

[3] *Virginia Woolf* (Norfolk, Conn., New Directions, 1942), pp. 63 ff.

[4] *James Joyce's Ulysses* (New York, Alfred A. Knopf, 1934), p. 172.

[5] *Pilgrimage* (New York, Alfred A. Knopf, 1938), I, 437.

[6] *Dorothy M. Richardson* (London, Joiner and Steele, 1931), pp. 5 ff.

[7] Joseph Warren Beach, *The Twentieth Century Novel: Studies in Technique* (New York, D. Appleton–Century, 1932), p. 387.

[8] In the work of one novelist at least (Conrad Aiken's *Blue Voyage* and *The Great Circle*), the image is frequently in psychoanalytical terms. Being thus once removed from life, the effect is tedious and unconvincing.

[9] *Axel's Castle* (New York, Scribner's, 1931), p. 20.

[10] The use of the symbol as leitmotif is considered in the section below on the use of patterns in stream-of-consciousness literature.

[11] Richard Kain, *Fabulous Voyager* (Chicago, University of Chicago Press, 1947), p. 260.

CHAPTER 4.

[1] It is this highly designed quality of stream-of-consciousness fiction which sets it apart from the formlessness and chaos of much other twentieth-century fiction, especially that which springs from the naturalistic novel of the late nineteenth century. This quality also aligns stream-of-consciousness fiction closely with the resurgence of classical methods in poetry and drama. The astounding thing is that in defeating chaos, stream-of-consciousness fiction essentially has chaos as its subject matter. Cf. T. S. Eliot's *Family Reunion* as a counterpart in the poetic drama.

[2] Especially: Stuart Gilbert, *James Joyce's Ulysses* (New York, Alfred A. Knopf, 1934); Richard M. Kain, *Fabulous Voyager* (Chicago, University of Chicago Press, 1947); and Harry Levin, *James Joyce: A Critical Introduction* (Norfolk, Conn., New Directions, 1941).

[3] This is taken from the tabulation in Gilbert, work cited, chap. ii.

[4] Harry Levin, work cited, p. 97.

[5] Frederick J. Hoffman, *Freudianism and the Literary Mind* (Baton Rouge, La., Louisiana State University Press, 1945), p. 133.

[6] For example, the *Don Giovanni* theme signaled by the "La ci

darem" motif. An ingenious presentation of this is to be found in an article by Vernon Hall, Jr., "Joyce's Use of Da Ponte and Mozart's *Don Giovanni," Publications of the Modern Language Association of America,* LXVI, 78.

[7] Gilbert's *Ulysses, passim,* and Frank Budgen's *James Joyce and the Making of Ulysses* (New York, H. Smith and R. Haas, 1934), pp. 15, 20, 39, establish conclusively Joyce's self-conscious intention.

[8] *The Odyssey,* Book X.

[9] Gilbert, *Ulysses,* p. 190.

[10] *The Making of Ulysses,* p. 20.

[11] Gilbert, work cited, chap. ii.

[12] *Ibid.,* p. 30.

[13] By Ellsworth G. Mason, "Joyce's *Ulysses* and the Vico Cycle" (Ph.D. dissertation, Yale University, 1948). The theories Joyce was attracted to are found in Vico's 1744 edition of *La Scienze Nuova.* See Gilbert, work cited, pp. 37–39 for Joyce's interest in Vico. For the influence of Vico's theories on *Finnegans Wake,* see Samuel Beckett, "Dante . . . Bruno. Vico . . . Joyce," *An Exagmination of James Joyce* by Beckett, *et al.* (Norfolk, Conn., New Directions, 1939), and Joseph Campbell and Henry Morton Robinson, *A Skeleton Key to Finnegans Wake* (New York, Harcourt, Brace, 1944), pp. 5 ff.

[14] "James Joyce et Pécuchet," *Polite Essays* (London, Faber and Faber, 1937).

[15] Joseph Warren Beach, *The Twentieth Century Novel: Studies in Technique* (New York, D. Appleton–Century, 1932), p. 418.

[16] Joan Bennett, *Virginia Woolf—Her Art as a Novelist* (London, Cambridge University Press, 1945), pp. 103–104.

[17] *Virginia Woolf* (Norfolk, Conn., New Directions, 1942), pp. 82 ff.

[18] *To the Lighthouse* (New York, Harcourt, Brace, 1927), p. 310.

[19] *Mrs. Dalloway,* Modern Library Edition (New York, Random House, 1928; copyright 1925 by Harcourt, Brace), p. 283.

[20] *The Sound and the Fury* and *As I Lay Dying,* Modern Library Edition (New York, Random House, 1930), p. 345.

[21] *Ibid.,* p. 19.

[22] *Ibid.,* p. 9.

[23] "William Faulkner," *Forms of Modern Fiction,* ed. William Van O'Connor (Minneapolis, University of Minnesota Press, 1948), pp. 125 ff.

[24] *A Portrait of the Artist as a Young Man,* in *Viking Portable Joyce* (New York, Viking, 1947), p. 471.

CHAPTER 5.

[1] (New York, Harcourt, Brace, 1946), p. 426.

[2] (New York, Random House, 1950), p. 258.

[3] Beach in *The Twentieth Century Novel: Studies in Technique* (New York, D. Appleton–Century, 1932); Hoffman in *The Modern Novel in America, 1900–1950* (Chicago, Regnery, 1951).